KITCHEN
CREATION

HOW TO PLAN AND BUY A FITTED KITCHEN

JANE ZACCARINI

MARTIN BOOKS

Published by Martin Books
Simon & Schuster International Group
Fitzwilliam House
32 Trumpington Street
Cambridge CB2 1QY

In association with
Tricity Bendix Ltd
Tricity Bendix House
55-59 High Road
Broxbourne
Herts EN10 7HJ

First published 1989
Text © Jane Zaccarini 1989
Illustrations © Woodhead-Faulkner
(Publishers) Ltd 1989
Copyright in the photographs belongs
to the following organisations, whose
help is gratefully acknowledged:

Tricity Bendix Ltd
Ideal Furniture Products Limited
Carron Stainless Products Limited
Franke UK Ltd
Plumb Center Limited

ISBN 0 85941 587 2

Design: Ken Vail Graphic Design
Illustrations: Richard Jacobs
& John Erwood
Printed and bound in Spain
by Graficas Estella, S.A.

ACKNOWLEDGEMENTS

The author and Publishers would
particularly like to thank
Ideal Furniture Products Ltd,
Dumbarton, for their help with the
photographs on the front cover, title
page and page 93.

The author would also like to thank
**Tricity Bendix Ltd, Kitchen Specialists
Association, Carron Stainless Products
Limited** and the **Plumb Center Limited**
for information supplied for this book.

Jane Zaccarini is a kitchen consultant
with Plumb Center Ltd. All views
expressed in this book are those of the
author and not necessarily of Tricity
Bendix Limited or Plumb Center Ltd.

To Erica Zaccarini and Mike John

CONTENTS

INTRODUCTION

You have decided to splash out on that much-needed, brand-new fitted kitchen – but where do you start? There is a lot to know about planning and buying kitchens, but this book aims to arm you with the full facts in a simple manner: I hope to prevent your dreams becoming sleepless nights!

Have you asked yourself why the kitchen is an important place? After all it is the very heart of the home, a very busy room and the focal point for everyday life. No longer is it the solitary cook's domain – it's a family room. It is also a room you don't consider refurbishing very often and, having decided to go ahead, you want to get it right. It would also be nice, in the process, to increase the value of your property!

With so many places selling fitted kitchens nowadays, shopping around and getting sound advice can be a nightmare. The average customer soon begins to feel they are wandering around aimlessly in a vast minefield of 'special offers', 'free' this and that; high-pressure salesmen and even unscrupulous con merchants. Indeed, they are. So, how to avoid the pitfalls? Planning and buying a new kitchen does not have to be complex: it can be easy. In fact it can even be fun! All you have to remember is to approach the situation calmly and in the correct sequence. Use your common sense. You must be logical and you must have a modicum of patience ... DON'T fall in love with the latest pink and green spotted doorfront ... DON'T rush to sign on the dotted line to save 10 per cent if you buy on the spot ... DON'T bite the salesman's hand off to take advantage of the 'free' gas hob, oven, worktops, wall units, and so on that he is offering ... Remember, it may be 8–10 weeks before the kitchen is completed.

Read this book, and then put on your thinking cap and your walking shoes and you are ready to go shopping. Good luck and have fun!

WHERE TO SHOP

First of all, let us look at the market as a whole and consider the various places where you can buy a fitted kitchen or kitchen units.

I think I am safe in saying that with fitted kitchens the British started the ball rolling – but how much American influence existed in the concept of a fitted kitchen is uncertain. Certainly English Rose were advertising fitted kitchens in the 1940s like that on page 4.

The market really took off in the late sixties and early seventies. F. W. Wrighton (now Wrighton International) were the first in the United Kingdom to produce a modern style of fitted kitchen, with the help of their designer, the late Nigel Walters. Then Hygena took up the idea, with their 'System 70' kitchen which was designed by George Fejer. It was Hygena who improved the basic concept and brought the fitted kitchen within the reach of the general public.

At the same time in Germany, the Germans, who had the advantage of a clean post-war sweep when setting up their manufacturing plants, geared themselves up with the latest equipment and began to produce and sell kitchens both at home and abroad. Here the forerunners were Poggenpohl and Siematic. In the main, the British manufacturer began by making his kitchens for 'on-the-shelf' stock, whereas the Germans made only for and specifically to order. At the present moment in the United Kingdom, the growth rate of the kitchen market is 10–15 per cent per annum, and 75–80 per cent of the market as a whole is taken by the British manufacturers. The remaining 20–25 per cent is still held by, for the major part, Germans, then the French and

finally the Italians. A cliché in the trade is that the British 'know the price of everything and the value of nothing'. You may take offence at that statement, but it is true that, on the whole, the average British consumer looks first at the price tag; whereas our continental counterparts look first at the quality of the goods they are about to buy, and the reputation of the people they are buying from. This British obsession with getting the lowest price can actually prevent the buyer from getting value for money.

The Kitchen Specialists Association says that, according to the Office of Fair Trading, in the course of 1985, (the last year for which figures are available) 215,000 people parted with £18 million in lost deposits in the home improvements market. Many of those 215,000 were victims of what have become known as 'kitchen cowboys'. I cannot stress too much the importance of being on your guard against inferior quality and disreputable practices.

There are now approximately 6,500 outlets in the United Kingdom selling kitchen units. In 1986 the value of kitchens sold through these outlets was an impressive £1,200 million. Around 20 per cent of kitchen retailers cease trading each year, many of them overnight; and thus, at the moment, the picture we have to paint is not an entirely pretty one. However, if you are armed with knowledge and with a little forethought, there is no reason why you should fall prey to the kitchen cowboys. There are lots of reputable outlets and this book will describe their advantages and disadvantages, so you will know what to look for.

First, however, some basic definitions. You need to be aware that there are

basically two different kinds of fitted kitchen: rigid construction and self-assembly. The names are self-explanatory and you will find a lengthier discussion of their characteristics on page 13–14.

You also need to be aware of what is meant by the name 'kitchen designer'. A kitchen designer is a glorified kitchen planner. Planning is the real word for it. Strictly speaking a kitchen designer should be a person who designs the units and doors, but they are a rare species: most times it's the men in the office who decide what is the colour and style this year, although some bigger manufacturers actually go to the trouble of doing market research to find out what colour and style the majority of customers prefer. Different types of outlet have different levels of kitchen planning services available, and you should be clear in your own mind what service you want and need and choose your shop accordingly.

Kitchen studios

First of all there are the up-market studios which really were the pioneers of the fitted kitchen in the United Kingdom. Studios sell mainly imported kitchens — German on the whole, French sometimes, and maybe Italian. Studios always have a designer who spends most of his or her time at a drawing board, producing breathtaking plans and perspective drawings designed to convince you that the kitchen you are about to buy, will, for its beauty, compete with the seven wonders of the world. Kitchen studios will normally fit the kitchen for you as part of the complete deal and your finished fitted kitchen will be of rigid construction and very well made; you can expect all sorts of pull-outs … push-ins … swing this and thats … all the built-in ovens and other appliances you could desire. It is worth remembering that you may have indirectly paid high foreign wages for the workmanship of the kitchen units and heavy transport costs to get it from the country of origin; this type of kitchen is never going to be cheap.

I must hastily add, however, that many good kitchen studios and specialists do exist, and that a good one will provide a really high-quality service, with great attention to detail. They will let you spend as long as you want in planning and be interested in the total look you want to achieve. For a really individual, creative approach to designing your dream kitchen, they are a good bet. Do consider them as a possibility if you can afford them and think their kind of service will suit you.

DIY stores

Next come the DIY stores, to be found in number in every part of the land. DIY stores do one of two things. They either manufacture their own units (self-assembly of course), or have a deal with a large British manufacturer, who produces their usual self-assembly kitchen units for the store, but with frontal finishes exclusive to that particular DIY outlet. The range of units you can buy here is usually fairly basic, though adequate to complete a fitted kitchen, and usually you can buy your oven, hob and other appliances with your units.

DIY stores may employ a member of staff who will help you with the planning of your kitchen, or indeed one who is trained to plan the kitchen for you. These plans will usually be on graph paper, in rough, and because the salesman/planner works on a commission basis in a busy store and tries to deal with as many customers as possible in the space of one day, you'll need to check-measure the plans for yourself. (There's no joy in fitting your own kitchen, when, on nearing completion you find that the worktops are too short, or you've two cupboards left over.) DIY shops don't offer the kind of kitchen planning expertise found in a specialist shop. You must have every detail clear in your own mind, a check-list that is completely comprehensive and be prepared to check and double-check everything when it arrives. On the other hand, DIY stores are not expensive, though a few do over-price their stock, and provided you have the right facts at the planning stage and do not particularly need to flaunt the name of your German Designer kitchen at dinner parties, and it is a reputable store, they are on the whole a good bet.

Kitchen shops

These are the smaller shops, usually in a run-down part of town, run single-handed by an ex-DIY or ex-Studio kitchen planner. The kitchens are usually of a lesser-known make from a minor British manufacturer, or a better-known brand bought through a distributor of kitchens, which of course makes them marginally more expensive. The shop will want to plan your kitchen and is usually in cahoots with a carpenter-cum-plumber-cum-electrician-and-tiler, who will install it. You may find the same kitchens here as in the DIY stores. (Different colours and knobs, of course!) Depending on whether or not the salesman is content with a little honest profit and knows his stuff, these, too, can be value for money. But beware! There is always the unscrupulous kitchen salesman who will delight in pressing an extra nought on his calculator and inflating the price of the worktops. After all, it would take an A-level in mathematics to work out the total price of the décor panel for your fridge at so much per square millimetre. So if it's an on-the-spot verbal sale (*not* recommended anyway) and you've nothing in writing, you've got to be good and quick to catch a con-man out.

Trading estate workshops

Another type of smaller outlet that seems to be springing up these days is the trading estate workshop outfit, this time usually owned and run by an ex-kitchen carpenter. This man is manufacturing his own kitchens on a small scale, and will, of course, install the kitchen for you, should you so require. Two potential disadvantages here: first of all, the carpenter's wife will have chosen the colours and styles available, which is all right if you like them too. Secondly, the general attitude to design, planning and installing will be based upon making life easy for the carpenter, and won't generally revolve around what you would like in your kitchen or how you would like it. In other words, not much thought may have been given to the aesthetics of the finished job. Provided you judge carefully the quality of the units (we'll come to that in the next chapter), you like the look of the kitchen doors, and you are, after shopping around, happy with the price, this may be the place for you. Here again, good and bad outlets exist.

Freelance carpenters

There does of course exist the higher class of carpenter; he is very often just a one-man-band. His units are solid wood through and through and he plans, makes specially and fits the kitchen with tailor-made units of non-specific sizes. This is fine if this is what you'd prefer, but usually made-to-measure kitchens will cost you the proverbial arm and leg and aren't often a testimony to the carpenter's planning and design capabilities, however good a wood-worker he may be. By the way, don't buy your appliances from a 'one-man-band', because he will have had to buy them from somewhere in the first place and will sell them to you at a marked-up price. By the time you've finished reading this book, you should be well equipped to choose and buy your own appliances with confidence, at the best possible prices.

Builders' merchants

Next we come to the builders' merchants, of which there are two types. First the smaller, back-street merchant, who'll only sell the odd sink base anyway, and secondly the larger chain of nationally owned builders' merchants. Most often it is the plumber or the carpenter who is their biggest customer, but they have opened their doors – with the advent of DIY – to the general public, and it may well pay you to call in and have a browse. Some of the staff may be trained in kitchen planning and larger merchants will be buying-in decent but inexpensive units direct from the manufacturer on a fairly large scale, and thus are in a position to compete with the DIY stores on price. If you make it clear that you are buying and fitting the kitchen yourself, you may even be able to talk discounts. (Wherever you go ask for discounts anyway: it can't do you any harm!) A few builders' merchants will also have access to rigid-construction kitchens, which are straight take-offs of the German ones you buy from kitchen studios, with all the gadgets and sophistication. These, however, will have been made in the United Kingdom and consequently will be half the price. Bully them into letting you put as much time and thought into the planning stage as you would at a studio and on the whole you've got a bargain. If you buy an even cheaper good-quality self-assembly kitchen with as much thought again, you're really onto a winner.

Direct-sell organisations

You may have realised that we have missed one very large sector of the kitchen market. Turn to any Sunday supplement and you will see lovely pictures of fitted kitchens, together with amazing offers and 'freebies'. These manufacturing and selling organisations recruit young high pressure salesmen, who will invade the privacy of your home, conjure up a plan and price on the spot and insist that you sign on the dotted line. Very often there will be finance deals available to you, too. Some of these people may indeed do a good job, who's to generalise? But I would be very wary of committing yourself to a deal before every little why and wherefore has been considered in your own good time.

Generally, direct-sell organisations are costly without being exorbitant. Their other big disadvantage is that their kitchens come from one central warehouse and are co-ordinated to arrive at the same time as the gang of workmen who have been sub-contracted to install the kitchen for you. Thus, if you are a vital screw short on the fearful day you could find yourself without water for a fortnight.

Fig 1.1 Kitchen planning with the aid of a computer may be available at some kitchen shops.

Who should plan your kitchen?

Earlier in this chapter I made mention of kitchen planning services which may be available to you where you buy your kitchen. I do feel that the best way to approach planning is by getting down to it yourself; and then, when you have a satisfactory or near-satisfactory solution, you can approach the kitchen planner who can cast a critical eye over your work, possibly come up with further suggestions or improvements, and generally tidy up any ragged ends you may have left. Bear in mind that if you do, in the final analysis, put the onus on the experts, then you will, in the event of errors, have some recourse, because final approval has been by the supplier.

If you do feel you want to take advantage of planning services, try to ascertain for what length of time the planner has actually been involved in planning kitchen layouts. A novice in the kitchen planning world can all too often make fatal mistakes by learning the ropes at your expense. You can also enquire if a planner is qualified, i.e. what courses he has attended and what certificates he holds. Most larger manufacturers provide short courses in kitchen planning – as do certain private institutes – and there are also a few recognised examination-based qualifications.

Incidentally, there are a few organisations who can give you advice or information about kitchens. There is the Kitchen Specialists Association and the Kitchen Information Service, both of whom are London-based. There is also the British Institute of Kitchen Architects in Crowborough, East Sussex.

Never mistake a salesman for a kitchen planner. He may be charming and polite in the showroom but you really ought to be more interested in the product he is offering and, in the case of planning, his drawing abilities, than how nicely he presents himself to you.

You may even want to enlist the help of a freelance planner who won't try to sell you anything but will merely plan your kitchen for a set fee. In the end, nobody is better qualified to plan your kitchen for you than you yourself, if you apply yourself correctly to the task in hand. After all, you live and work there and you should determine what you do and do not want.

It's worth mentioning that some kitchen sellers may use a computer as an aid to kitchen planning. These computers are very clever because they can draw pictures too. But as far as the actual planning goes, they are only as good as the person who programmed the computer and the person operating it. They are good for meticulous check-measuring of a plan.

Finance

When considering taking out a loan for the purpose of home improvements, you should assess your financial position carefully. There are two methods of arranging finance that are commonly used for the purpose of home improvements.

Secured loans
If you take out a secured loan, your home is used as collateral security. You could approach the bank or building society with whom you have your current mortgage and apply for a further advance. Your application would be considered in a similar way to that of a normal mortgage application. Normally, this would require confirmation of your ability to repay the additional loan and an up-to-date valuation of your property. It is common for the further advance to be arranged in such a way that the term of your loan would coincide with the ultimate repayment of your main mortgage.

Even if you do not currently have a mortgage on your property, that is you own it outright, this type of loan may still be available; you should approach a bank or building society for details of their lending policies.

It is unlikely that a solicitor would need to be employed for the purpose of arranging a further advance, except in the case of an applicant who does not have a current mortgage.

Unsecured loans
In this case you apply to a bank or finance company. They will consider your application purely on your ability to repay and your credit history to date. It is very important to compare interest rates offered by finance companies as they can vary considerably. Some types of fitted kitchen outlets, especially if they are also fitting the kitchen for you, may offer their own finance package in association with a finance company. It is still worth shopping around to see if you get a better deal from other finance companies or banks. Don't waste the effort you put into shopping around to get the best deal for your kitchen by making a less-than-intelligent appraisal of the various finance options.

In the short term, you will probably find that the secured loan method will carry lower monthly repayment costs, but remember that you will probably need to make repayments of the loan for the duration of your main mortgage. Therefore, in the long term you may find that the overall cost is greater than an unsecured loan. Generally, the interest rates for unsecured loans are higher than those for secured loans, but it may suit your purpose to make higher repayments in the short term in order to ensure earlier repayment.

Unsecured loans tend to be repayable over a period of 3–10 years, but it is possible to arrange such loans over a longer period. When calculating the cost of your monthly repayments, do remember that Income Tax relief is not allowable for home improvement loans.

In conclusion

Don't be confused. Absorb the facts before you go and decide which operation is the one you would prefer, or try a few to see how it goes. One final work of advice first: don't go from pillar to post obtaining plans and quotes from all and sundry, or you will end up much more confused and doubtful than when you started looking. Plump for two or even three bona fide firms and get brochures and price lists to scrutinise by the fireside at leisure. After all the average house only gets its kitchen done every twenty years or so, so you want to do it right and you do, above all, want a nicely planned kitchen that reflects the best possible value for your money: this is, in the end, what it is all about.

Check-list: where to buy your kitchen

	Kitchen studios	DIY stores	Kitchen shops	Trading estate workshops	Freelance carpenters	Builder's merchants	Direct sell organisations
Imported or British	Imported	🇬🇧	Both	🇬🇧	🇬🇧	🇬🇧	🇬🇧
Fitting	✓	✗	✓	✓	✓	✗	✓
Rigid or self-assembly	Rigid	Self-assembly	Both	Both	Rigid made-to-measure	Both, usually self-assembly	Self-assembly
Appliances sold with units	✓	✓	✓	✓	✗	✓	✓
Good range of accessories	✓	✗	✗	✗	✗	✗	✓
Price	££££	££	£	£££	£££	£	£££
Kitchen planning service	✏✏✏✏✏	✏	✏✏✏	✏✏	✏	✏	✏✏✏
Range of units	★★★★★	★★★	★★★	★★	★	★	★★

CHOOSING YOUR UNITS: WHAT TO LOOK FOR

We have ascertained that there are innumerable makes of kitchen units on the market; before I set you on course for the shops, let me familiarise you with the way in which kitchen units are made and what they are made of. Most of you will be in for a few surprises.

Before I embark, let me make it clear that all these different sorts of kitchen units cost all sorts of different money and it doesn't always follow that the more you pay the better off you will be. There are good cheap kitchens and bad expensive ones.

I intend to arm you with enough information to make you a mini-expert. Certainly by the the time you've finished this chapter you will know more than the average salesman; or perhaps I should say that you'll know more than the average salesman is prepared to let on.

Materials

The first surprise: nowadays nearly all kitchen carcases, that is, the cupboard itself and not the door, are made not of wood, but of chipboard. Chipboard is a board produced by compressing chips of wood and glue. Make no mistake: when a salesman or an advertisement tells you how wonderful a solid oak kitchen is, he or it is talking about the doors and not the whole unit. If you really do want a solid wood kitchen through and through you'll have to get a carpenter to make it especially for you.

So, a cupboard (called a unit), which comprises a carcase and a door or 'frontal', is a box of a given size made of chipboard which has been coated in melamine plastic (MFC). The melamine plastic is the important part, because it is what stops the water in the kitchen getting into the chipboard and causing it to swell, and therefore warp, crack and disintegrate.

Of course, there are different qualities of chipboard, that is, different densities of chippings and different thicknesses of finished board. Unless you are truly an expert you won't be able to tell how dense a board is, since it is completely covered by the melamine plastic; you will be able to see, in the showroom, the thickness of the board and how well the ends are finished.

A good pointer to the quality of the materials used is whether the units carry a guarantee. Many are guaranteed for five years; some, and even some of the cheaper ones, are guaranteed for twenty years. You can, of course, be cheeky and ask the salesman from what density of chipboard his kitchen units are constructed. He'll think you are a 'clever dick', and probably won't even know. (If by any remote chance he does, it's full marks to him.) In any event he's not going to tell you that they're not dense or strong enough, so it's best just to ask him what sort of guarantee he can offer.

The kitchen you are thinking of purchasing may be what is called a 'rigid' kitchen, or a 'self-assembly' kitchen. The latter is often also referred to as 'flat-pack' or 'knock-down'. Both types are made of the same materials in the same way. Self-assembly kitchens are a British invention and made solely in the United Kingdom. The units are in parts, packed into boxes and delivered to you to assemble and fit. Rigid units are assembled in the factory and arrive ready-made-up, to be simply slotted into place.

There are, have been, and always will be arguments about the advantages and disadvantages of rigid versus self-assembly kitchens. I'll point out a few of the why's and wherefores and let you make up your own mind.

Fig 2.1 A good-quality self-assembly kitchen can be very glamorous and is not hard to put together.

Self-assembly kitchens

Self-assembly units, because they are packed in flat boxes, are easy to store, so there shouldn't be much of a wait between placing an order and delivery of the kitchen units. The longest you can expect to wait for this type of kitchen is ten days. Worktops will be in set lengths, called 'blanks', up to a maximum of 3.5 metres long.

You will have noticed that I have started to use metric terms. This is a must. THINK METRIC! If you wander about thinking in feet and inches and converting everything as you go along with the help of a tape measure, a pencil and the back of a cigarette packet, you will, I guarantee, end up in a terrible mess. More about tips on thinking metric later. Your self-assembly kitchen won't be expensive, and you can save on delivery charges by collecting it, a load at a time if necessary, in the family runabout. (You will need a roof rack for worktops though.) It is always worth asking the store if they offer a free delivery service. If planned well and correctly fitted, a self-assembly kitchen can be every bit as glamorous as a rigid one.

Remember, though, that if you are paying a carpenter he will automatically charge you more to put together self-assembly units than he will merely to slot rigid units into place. Don't let the thought of assembly put you off if you intend to fit the kitchen yourself. Assembly is very easy and in most cases

step-by-step illustrated instructions are provided with each unit. I have put a good self-assembly unit together in ten minutes, and I'm a weaker sex member and a stranger to the screwdriver as well. I know one carpenter who averages four minutes per unit and gets it right first time round every time.

On the other hand, I have come across self-assembly instructions that might as well have been written in Greek; if yours are like these, this can cause you a major headache. It may help, if you are genuinely considering a particular self-assembly kitchen, and want to fit it yourself, to ask to look at the instructions in advance, just to make sure you will be able to follow them.

Backs of the units
Just a quick word about the backs of the units. Manufacturers sometimes save a bob or two by omitting them. Most units, even more expensive ones, will have hardboard backs, some will have, believe it or not, half a back. Check in the showroom that, when the unit is assembled, the backs of them are indeed in existence and that they are fairly firm and rigid.

Fixings of the units
Inspect also the fixings of the units. Very cheap units are often assembled with woodscrews driven into special chipboard plugs. Plastic caps are then used to conceal the heads of the screws. In better-quality units, cam-locking fixings are used, which are very strong.

Adjustable feet
Another good feature to look for is adjustable feet that support the unit and are hidden by the bottom plinth. They make it easier to level the unit at the point of fitting and accommodate uneven floors. They also add strength of support.

Rigid-construction kitchens

Rigid kitchens, because they have been assembled in the factory, are bulky, cost more to manufacture and transport and therefore are usually more expensive than the self-assembly type. They are also normally made to order and the waiting period for them can be anything from 5–10 weeks. Because they are made to order, there is a larger variety of sizes and types of units available and some companies will even make 'specials' to your own requirements, at an extra cost.

With rigid units, the worktops provided are usually ordered cut to size exactly, with mitre cuts for the corners and cut-outs for hobs and sinks. A word of warning: it is fairly difficult to plan a tailor-made worktop with cut-outs correct to the millimetre, which is what they need to be, so you are best advised to buy over-sized lengths of worktop and cut them to suit on site in the kitchen. More about worktops later!

Rigid-construction kitchens should always be supplied with full, firmly-attached back panels, good quality fittings and adjustable feet; do check for these things in the shop.

When properly planned a rigid kitchen is a sophisticated improvement to one's home, and certainly, if you do indeed hanker after all those 'push-ins' and 'pull-outs', swing shelves and carousel cupboards as mentioned in the previous chapter, then this type of kitchen is probably the one for you. If you intend to pay a carpenter to fit the kitchen, then the extra you will pay for the units you will gain back on the price of carpentry, since less labour is involved.

Other considerations

The best general approach when weighing up the quality of the units is to look at them carefully and decide for yourself if they are well made, strong and solid. After a couple of examinations of different units you will soon get the idea.

Colour may be worth mentioning here. The inside of the unit will usually be beige or white, and the outsides of the carcase the same colour, though for some unfathomable reason, sometimes the insides and outsides don't match. I've come across heartbroken housewives who have found that their lovely new all-white kitchen has beige cupboard insides, or vice versa. Again, do check.

The kitchens on display in shops and showrooms, may, for example, have an oak door and beige insides, and all the visible exterior ends may be finished in an oak-effect material to match the doors. If the kitchen is priced or you are quoted a price, you may find that the price includes units with beige or white external ends and that oak finishes on unit exterior sides are extra. Some places may conveniently forget to tell you this and then you are going to be vastly disappointed with the finished overall effect, or you may have an extra bill for oak-effect ends. Make it clear from the start what you would prefer and what you can afford or want to pay. In other words, when buying, dot your i's and cross your t's.

The doors of your units

Now we come to the doors. This is a question of personal taste, often dictated by fashion. A particular door design may catch your eye, but look closely at how well it is made and finished, and try to judge for yourself why one particular door should cause a kitchen to be more expensive than another, since the same range of units will carry different price labels, depending solely upon the different doors.

There are a variety of different types of doors. First, laminated chipboard, second, painted chipboard, and third, wood. There are two types of wood doors, solid and veneer.

Laminated doors
Laminated doors come plain, or with wooden trims which may serve as a type of handle. Laminate is made from sheets of paper that are impregnated with resins and subjected to great pressure and heat until the material fuses into a thin sheet of great durability. Laminates are extremely tough and can withstand the detrimental effects of water, sunlight and domestic cleaners and also will withstand temperatures of up to 150°C, so they are not to be sniffed at. Melamine is sometimes used as a cheaper alternative to laminates.

Painted doors
Painted doors are as good as the paint that is used on them. This ranges from a simple cellulose spray to a high gloss of extremely durable polyester resin paint. A good trick is to take a coin and rub it hard on the surface of the door (ask permission first!). This trick applies to laminated doors as well as painted ones. If the coin marks, you know where you stand. If it doesn't, the product should stand up to general wear and tear.

Wood doors

Wood doors are mainly made of oak; sometimes mahogany or pine; and occasionally chestnut or other lesser-known woods. Oak is by far the favourite. Pine is a very soft wood and will, in time, get very tatty, because it marks easily. Your 'country kitchen' look should be achieved with light oak and not pine, if possible.

Oak can be spray-coloured light, medium or dark, in all the various permutations. Mahogany is a reddish wood, spray-stained to be even redder brown than it would be naturally. Chestnut is exactly as the name suggests and there are lighter and darker versions. Pine is always a light colour, tending to yellow.

I have already issued a warning about 'solid wood' kitchens and we have ascertained that 'solid' applies to the doors only. We can now talk about them in a little more detail.

There are solid wood doors and there are veneered wood doors. Either consists of a frame with a panel in the middle. The frame is solid and the panel is either solid and carved out to give a sculptured look or veneered, that is, a flat sheet of veneer is glued and tacked into the framework. If a sculptured look is achieved with veneer panels, one panel is glued on top of another in a variety of shapes.

Again, ask! It is against the Trade Descriptions Act to sell a veneer as a solid oak, though some companies try to get around that by saying that the frames are solid. Listen carefully to what the salesman has to say. It is a fairly simple matter to compare a solid carved door panel to a flatter veneered one. You'll catch on after you have inspected a few.

Hinges

An important feature of the unit that needs to be looked at is the hinges. They must be strong and fit well in a sturdy manner to the carcase and the door. They are all that is holding the carcase and the door together, so they must be strong.

I've come across people who wouldn't look at a kitchen twice unless it had 180-degree hinges, which allow the door to be opened right back on itself, flat against the row of units, but others have complained that their 180-degree hinges kept malfunctioning and breaking. Ninety-degree hinges are the norm nowadays and these will allow the door to open until it is at right angles to the unit front, which is of course adequate for access into the unit.

I think there is a case for 180-degree hinges when there are a number of boisterous young children or animals in the household, as either may run into an open 90-degree door, damaging the hinge and possibly themselves. I am not convinced, however, that the average couple are so slap-happy and harassed that they can't open and shut cupboard doors properly so as to avoid accidents, not only to life and limb, but to the units. In addition, hinges are mostly spring-loaded to stop the door being left ajar. Here again ask about a guarantee: if your kitchen is guaranteed and the hinges give up the ghost, you are entitled to get them replaced. So a manufacturer who guarantees his kitchens should be fairly certain of the lifespan of his hinges.

Handles

Handles come in various shapes and sizes — knob; D-shaped; fancy drop — or as an integral part of the door trim. Try the handles a few times to see that they are nice and easy to use. Try and do this as if you are in a hurry, because you may find that after a few times you'll find it easier to grab the edge of the door rather than the handle. If this is the case the design is poor and you'll end up with sticky finger marks on the edges of the doors in your kitchen. Fancy drop handles can be a pain too, because they may drop against the door after use and can scratch and mark the wood or paint after a while.

Drawers

Next we come to the drawers, that is, what is called the drawer-box. Long-gone are the days when drawer-boxes were made of wood: don't expect it. I am afraid you will have to content yourself with plastic or hardboard, or a mixture of both. Moulded plastic drawers are preferable to hardboard ones, and concealed runners (i.e., ones you can't see when you pull out the drawer) are best. Pull out and push in the drawers several times and see how they fare. If they are good, they will feel good, and if they are bad, they will stick and falter and feel bad. There is a world of difference and you will easily be able to tell if the drawers are bad. Next take the drawer-box completely out of the unit and inspect it. Does it look and feel strong and well made? Pay special attention to where the drawer-front is attached to the drawer-box. This is an extremely weak point on poorer quality kitchens. I once knew a salesman who used to delight in putting the drawer-box upside-down on the showroom floor and stamping on it to show how strong it was. I don't recommend you do this but you should bear in mind that a good, honest salesman will have every faith in his product, and should be grateful for a customer who shows an enlightened and informed interest. A sign of a reputable outlet is how willingly and fully they will answer your questions.

Worktops

Just as the major part of your kitchen will be made of chipboard, worktops also are chipboard, with a laminate covering. You don't necessarily have to get your worktops from the same manufacturer from whom you buy your units. You don't even have to buy your worktops in the same place. Here again there are good and bad. Extremely cheap worktops are made from a low-density chipboard, with a comparatively thin laminate covering. I've known instances where ordinary coffee cups caused rings on the surface of cheaper worktops; and I've also come across worktops in which layers of newspaper were used to bulk out the chipboard. Buy a brand-name worktop and again, go for a guarantee.

Worktops come in two thicknesses, 30 mm thick and 40 mm thick, and are sold in 'blanks' 3 metres or 3.5 metres long. Very generally, the thicker the worktop the better. An average kitchen will use two of these blanks. The old square-edged worktop is very much a thing of the past. These days, there is a choice of bullnose edgings, wood-edged (for wooden kitchens), and postformed edgings.

Bullnose edgings look smart, but I've seen sinks underneath completely destroyed by water because water has continually run all round the bullnose edge and on to the doors of the units.

Wood-edged worktops have their disadvantages, too. They look nice because the edge matches the wooden trims on doors; however, their weakness lies in the fact that the wooden trim will, after years of use, tend to come away from the actual worktop. Here too, water is the main culprit. If you do decide on wood-edged worktops, buy them from the same place as the units, to ensure a perfect colour match.

Wood-edged worktops also come in the form of wood-edged boards designed for tiling. This is the most costly form of worktop, in terms of both materials and labour. If you do choose this type, use mosaic tiles because they'll break less easily and also use a special waterproof grout that will be hygienic. Such a grout is readily available.

Postformed worktops are the best design, because they are made like bullnose worktops, with integral curved edges, but, provided the underneaths of the tops are sealed the water will run straight off the bottom edge and onto the floor. Incidentally, always seal your worktops on every possible raw chipboard edge, and if you are employing a carpenter, insist he does this too. When ordering the tops, make sure that you include edging strips or that they are included automatically with the tops. These are used for finishing cut raw ends of worktops, when the top is cut to suit on site.

When choosing worktops in a showroom ask yourself the following questions:

1) Is it easy to keep clean?
2) Is the covering hard enough to resist scratching?
3) Is the covering heatproof?

By now you are indeed a mini-expert and you are probably going to enjoy your shopping expedition rather more because you can put your new-found knowledge to good use. Use the following check-list to weigh up the kitchens which you take a liking to. The completed check-list, plus any literature about the kitchen obtained in the shop or showroom, can then be studied at leisure. Having also compared prices, you can move onto looking at and thinking about your appliances.

To evaluate prices, always compare like with like. Take the price of a 1000 mm base and a 1000 mm wall standard unit for example, and look at what they cost in the different ranges. This should give you, at this stage, an inkling of the comparative costs of your units.

Fig 2.2 Upstand makes worktops easier to clean and more hygienic.

If if you wish to use ... tween the wall and ... back.

... the worktop easier ... ygienic: crumbs and ... t trapped between ... ksurface if you use ... an extra guarantee ... ep into the ... ck edge.

What to look for: a check-list

- ❖ ... he guarantee cover in ... isks?
- ❖ ... guarantee?
- ❖ ... id construction units?
- ❖ ... delivery?
- ❖ ... terior?
- ❖ ... colour exterior?
- ❖ Extra charge for wood-effect ends?

- ❖ Do the units have backs?
- ❖ Are they firmly attached?
- ❖ What type of fixings are used?
- ❖ Adjustable feet?
- ❖ Is there a good range of accessories?
- ❖ Type of door (laminate, painted, wood)?
- ❖ Solid wood or veneered doors?
- ❖ Free delivery?
- ❖ Delivery charges?

- ❖ Are self-assembly instructions clear?
- ❖ Quality of hinges?
- ❖ Type of hinges (90-degree, 180-degree)?
- ❖ Quality of drawer-boxes?
- ❖ Well designed handles?
- ❖ Quality of worktop?
- ❖ Style of worktop edging?
- ❖ Upstand?
- ❖ Comparative prices of units?

MARTIN'S KITCHEN PLANNING SCALE RULE 1:20

CHOOSING APPLIANCES FOR YOUR KITCHEN

The term 'household appliances' covers all electrical and gas equipment which you will be buying and installing with your kitchen units. Included under this umbrella term are: ovens, hobs, extractor fans, refrigerators, freezers, dishwashers, washing machines and tumble dryers.

You may be thinking of buying some, any or all of these types of appliances, and just as there are bad, good and better kitchen units, so there are many makes and qualities of appliances. However, unlike kitchen units, the adage 'you get what you pay for' is apt here. For example, a basic sum of money will buy a basic oven and a more princely sum will provide you with a very sophisticated one, if this is what you want.

Here again the Germans were the first to mass-market popular built-in appliances; they were swiftly followed by the Italians, who produced cheaper versions. We British have 'caught up' though; you won't do much better than to buy British nowadays. Foreign appliances are really only sought after now for their snobbery-value or their cheapness, depending upon where they are made. You won't get more for your money by buying imported goods.

In the bad old days when British kitchens were making their début, British built-in ovens and hobs were large, ugly and badly sized in relation to the units in which they were housed. Oven technology was behind the times and, because the manufacturers were taken by surprise by an influx of continental ovens, there was also a lack of communication and co-ordination between the kitchen unit manufacturers and the makers of the appliances.

The latter is still sometimes true, but not so much so that, armed with a little knowledge, it is impossible for the customer to cope. Some of the old built-in monstrosities still remain in people's kitchens as testimony to the development of modern appliances, but by now the majority of these appliances will be on their last legs, and the time has come to replace them with something more streamlined and better designed. There are plenty of good appliances around nowadays, and it can be a struggle to choose between them.

Ovens

An oven is essentially a metal box containing heating elements. The three types available are: built-in, built-under and slot-in. All types are available powered by gas or electricity. Gas ovens are usually dearer (though gas hobs are marginally cheaper than electric ones).

Built-in ovens

The built-in variety has been popular from the start. As the name implies they are built into a specially designed tall housing unit. They may be single or double ovens. They may also be built into brickwork.

The double oven has been more popular than the single. It is really a one-and-a-half oven: you can get hold of a double oven with two ovens of equal size, but really they are better adapted to catering kitchens. So when I refer to a double oven, I am talking about a one-and-a-half oven as illustrated opposite.

Sizes of double ovens are reasonably well standardised these days, and size is very important, as it must fit into the unit that houses it. All are designed to fit into a unit 600 mm wide, and the most popular size height-wise is 878 mm. Don't worry about the odd millimetre or so, and if you are still thinking in feet and inches, when you look on a metric tape you will soon realise that half a millimetre is to be sneezed at.

Don't worry too much about depth, either, as these are all standard too. Most kitchen unit manufacturers make their tall units to suit the standard size double oven, so if a double oven is the type you want, and kitchen space permits, try to choose a standard size and you will save yourself one headache. Consider here that only manufacturers of the rigid type of kitchen units will provide for a larger variety of sizes of ovens heightwise, and that the majority of self-assembly unit manufacturers do not provide a tall unit for a built-in single oven.

If you are considering self-assembly units and you want a single or odd-size oven, it is possible, if you enlist a good carpenter, to 'butcher' the height of the aperture of the unit, provided that it is larger than the oven, and fill in the gaps with what the trade call an 'infill'. However, to save yourself time and trouble, stick to what is standard and you won't go far wrong.

Electric double ovens are more common than gas, but double gas ovens are available; moreover, having an electric oven does not mean you cannot have a gas hob, or vice versa. Weigh up the advantages of having both gas and electric in your kitchen. There is something to be said for it in a powercut!

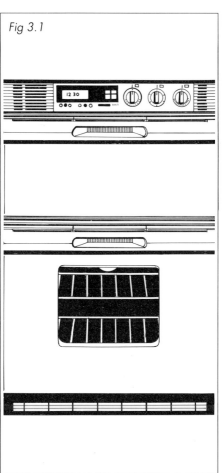

Fig 3.1

Fig 3.2

Fig 3.1 Built-in double oven

Fig 3.2 Built-in single oven

Fig 3.3 Standard double oven housing unit, with dimensions

Fig 3.4 This single oven is too small to fit into the aperture in a standard housing, so the housing unit has been 'butchered' to take it. The top and bottom cupboards are standard, but the middle 'door' is a decorative laminated sheet to match the doors and cover the remaining aperture.

Fig 3.5 Double ovens can be built into brickwork instead of a housing unit

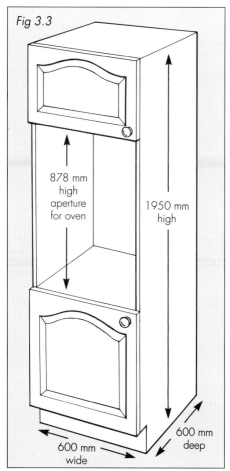

Fig 3.3

878 mm high aperture for oven

1950 mm high

600 mm wide

600 mm deep

Fig 3.4

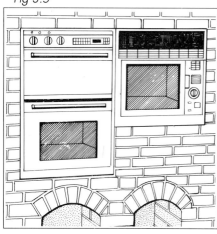

Fig 3.5

Built-under ovens

A built-under oven is a single oven, whether gas or electric, designed to be built into a 'built-under oven housing unit', under the worktop, usually with the hob over the top. Most of these ovens are electric; the main drawback is that they don't have a separate grill, but they have two advantages. Firstly, they need less kitchen space. A built-in oven and hob require at least 1500 mm of kitchen space, because as well as the 600 mm each needed for the oven housing and hob you need to plan in a 30 mm space between them. Otherwise the heat from the hob may scorch the side of the oven housing; you will find working at the hob very cramped and you will not be able to turn pan handles to the outside on the rings nearest the oven. A built-under oven only needs a minimum of 600 mm if the hob is placed directly over the oven, on the other hand. Single built-under ovens are now becoming more popular than built-in ovens.

Secondly, if you want a completely projection-free hob, without controls, so that the hob surface can be wiped over all at once, the built-under oven is the type to choose, because here the hob controls can in fact be on the oven rather than on the hob itself, whereas with a built-in oven the hob is sited at a distance from the oven and thus requires its own controls.

Moneywise, the cheapest combination is the electric built-under oven with controls combined with a gas or electric hob with its own controls.

Slot-in ovens

If you've a tiny kitchen and need to save space by using a single built-under oven but want a separate grill, perhaps you should consider a 'slot-in' oven. This is really an up-to-date version of your old cooker and doesn't need a housing. It slots into either a 500 mm or 600 mm space, and the height is usually adjustable to correspond to the height of your worktop. There is a wide choice of slot-in cookers on the market, and do just check the sizing before you think of planning one into your kitchen. One advantage of slot-in ovens is that they can be taken with you when you move house. They are also useful if you are replacing kitchen units but want to get more use out of your existing cooker, because old freestanding ovens are nearly all less than 600 mm wide, so you can plan a space of 600 mm, use your old oven, and put in a slot-in cooker at a later date. If you want an extractor fan over your slot-in oven, one manufacturer makes a 500 mm wide one, as well as the standard 600 mm size, so you could buy a 500 mm oven. Do be aware, though, that cooker hood wall units in the smaller size are not very common, so check if one is available in your chosen range before you start.

One thing to beware of here is that some slot-in ovens have lift up lids. Check that when the lid is raised it doesn't interfere with the extractor fan or the extractor fan unit above it.

One version of the slot-in oven with a separate grill uses a separate hob, this time set into the worktop. This would be one way of solving a space problem, achieving a built-in look, and having a separate grill at the same time.

Fig 3.6 Slot-in oven

Fig 3.7 Some slot-in cookers have lift up lids

Special oven features

There are many refinements to basic oven design available these days. The electric fan oven is very popular. An electric fan oven has elements behind a fan at the back of the oven. The elements heat the air, which is forced into the oven through a fan that also circulates the hot air around the oven. Thus the oven heats up quickly, and the warm air in the oven is evenly distributed. You can cook equally well in any part of the oven, and on more than one shelf at once, and this means no more lopsided cakes or part-browned pies. Fan oven cooking also requires marginally lower cooking temperatures, therefore saving on electricity also.

A much cheaper and certainly less satisfactory version of the fan oven is available. Here we have a conventional oven assisted by a fan, but this time the fan does not force the hot air through ducts into the oven, but merely ineffectively fans an already hot oven. So make sure your fan oven is not a poor imitation of the real thing!

Double fan ovens consist of a main fan oven and a smaller conventional oven, which usually doubles as a grill. Some ovens have added features such as rotisseries and meat probes. Remember that every added feature will undoubtedly add to the price.

Whilst looking at ovens, not only should you consider what practical features they have which you would like, but also take note of the design features. Some have doors which open to one side, and some have drop-down doors. Drop-down doors make good resting stations when taking a hot dish out of the oven, whereas side-opening doors mean you don't have to lean over to get into the oven. Consider which you would prefer and which one you would be more comfortable with.

Consider various features when inspecting built-under ovens too. For example, you will need to bend down to get at a built-under oven, and the grill and oven will be in the same compartment so you won't be able to grill and roast at the same time. Ask yourself what you are and are not happy about with your present oven or other ovens you have used. Decide for yourself what is best for you.

A feature of most modern ovens is that they incorporate timing devices of one kind or another. Some of these timing devices can be so fiddly to set that you'll never actually bother with them in the long run. Basic timing devices work on rollers. The clock can either be a conventional clock face or a digital-type display. Both types are set by turning knobs which work the roller mechanism.

Much easier to use are the electronic push button timing devices, so if you have decided that you need a timer, this is the type to go for, and it will be worth spending the extra money to get one.

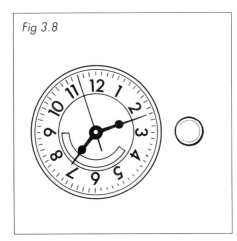

Fig 3.8

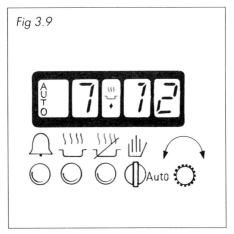

Fig 3.9

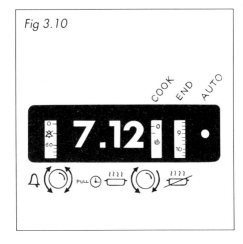

Fig 3.10

Fig 3.8 Clock face
roller mechanism timer

Fig 3.9 Digital display
roller mechanism timer

Fig 3.10 Electronic push-button timer

Do make sure, whilst looking at timing devices, that they actually switch the oven on *and* off. Some will only switch the oven on, which is no good if you have a puncture on the way home, as the oven continues to cook away merrily until the house burns down. Some will only switch it off, which means that if you want the casserole ready on your return from work, you have to nip out of the office to turn the oven on at the correct time, which defeats the whole object of having timing devices. Also, plump for a 24-hour timing control rather than a 12-hour one, or you won't be able to cook the Christmas turkey overnight.

Microwave ovens

Built-in microwaves are now readily available and there is a variety to choose from. I do not intend to talk at length about microwaves in general since there are plenty of excellent books available to which you may refer. Generally, my own experience of microwave ovens is that they are a boon, and can save time and energy by way of instant cooking that doesn't create a lot of washing up. There is no excuse for relegating your microwave to the tasks of defrosting, baking spuds and reheating cold food. With experimentation you will soon learn to use your microwave at all times during the day, and it *is* possible, in extreme circumstances, to substitute, a microwave for a conventional hob and oven. Certainly pay no attention to old wives' tales of escaping rays cooking people instead of food. I was once assured that microwaved food could cause cancer, which is one of many scandalous stories which have amused me since the advent of microwave cooking.

Be careful with sizing when building in a microwave, and never imagine that you can build an ordinary free-standing microwave into a housing unit. You need a microwave that has been specially designed to be built in. However, some are multi-purpose and designed to be freestanding on your worktop, or, with the aid of a 'build in kit', which is a type of frame, to be housed in a unit. Check the sizing on the manufacturer's brochures carefully. They will tell you what size aperture your housing unit must have to suit your microwave. One clever manufacturer has designed an 'all-in-one' single oven with a microwave on top; together these fit snugly in the standard 878 mm high space.

Do remember overall, that microwave oven technology is changing very rapidly and that you are likely to want to update what you have more frequently than other appliances. And whatever microwave you buy, do get it serviced regularly by a local microwave centre.

Hobs

There has been a vast improvement in hob technology in recent years and you will have lots of choice when you browse. Four-ring electric hobs and four-ring gas hobs are the biggest sellers. Also available are hobs with two gas and electric rings combined. Remember that they will be more expensive and inconvenient to plan in and install, because they need to be connected to both supplies. There are smaller, separate two-ring only hobs as well.

Some electric hobs have 'simmer stats' designed to prevent liquids boiling over, and are worth a mention. Whilst you are considering hobs, you may want to consider related equipment such as built-in griddles or deep-fat-fryers, which can also be set into the worktop.

Do be aware that the hob will be cut into the worktop and that worktops are usually 30 or 40 mm thick. Find out, therefore, if the hob is 'slimline'. A slimline hob will save a headache when you get to the planning stage because you won't have to worry about what you can fit in underneath it as it only takes up the depth of the worktop.

Ceramic hobs

A lot of keep-clean fanatics like the idea of ceramic hobs, because these can be easily wiped over after use. With ceramic hobs you need to be even more aware of the 'slimline' problem – and be aware, too, that they are twice the price of an ordinary hob.

Two newer additions to the range of ceramic hobs available are the halogen hob and the induction hob.

Halogen hobs

Halogen hobs cook by light. They are very impressive because they react so quickly to the control buttons that they are nearly as fast as gas. They work by using tungsten halogen lamps which create infra-red light – so the hob is heated at the speed of light. When looking at halogen hobs, be aware that the hob will usually have a combination of electric and ceramic rings and that you may choose to have one, two, three or all four halogen rings, depending upon price.

Induction hobs

Induction hobs do not involve direct heat. The heat is induced magnetically by the creation of a magnetic field, and the hob heats as quickly as a gas one. The ceramic surface of the hob stays cool whilst you are cooking and at the same time heat is induced in the base of the pan. Incidentally, for the hob to work it follows that the pots and pans you use must be magnetic, e.g. iron or steel, etc. and not ceramic or glass.

All three types of ceramic hobs need to have a warning light to show you when the hob is on, because otherwise there may be some nasty accidents; you can't tell when a ceramic hob is on just by looking at the cooking rings. One that stays on for a while after the heat is switched off could stop you burning yourself on a ring that is still hot. As with ovens, the more sophisticated the features of the hob, the more money you will have to part with.

Fig 3.11

Fig 3.11 Induction hob

Fig 3.12 Ceramic hob

Fig 3.13 Halogen hob

Fig 3.14 A hob warning light is a very useful safety device.

Control panels

If you want a completely projection-free hob, as an alternative to mounting the controls on a built-under oven under the hob as described on page 20, consider having a separate control panel for the hob. Control panels may be set in the worktop, under the worktop or into the wall. I have even seen controls set into a canopy which housed the extractor fan above the hob. Remember that separate control panels are an extra expense to be added to your final list of requirements.

Fig 3.12

Fig 3.13

Fig 3.14

Extractor fans

You may or may not decide to incorporate an extractor fan over your hob or oven. Extractor fans all do the same job of extracting steam, and consequently smells, from the hob area. There are several different styles of fans, (which are often referred to as 'hoods').

A basic extractor fan is designed to sit under a 600 mm 'cooker hood wall unit', which is slightly less tall than a standard wall unit. 500 mm extractor fans are available from one manufacturer: check that a wall unit in the same width is available.

The same style is sometimes available in the large size of 1000 mm, which again sits under a special wall unit. Also available nowadays are slimline telescopic hoods, which look very smart. These, too, have a cooker hood wall unit above them.

An 'integrated extractor fan' also uses 600 mm of space over the hob, but this time sits hidden behind a cupboard door or has a panel on the front to disguise it totally.

When you open the door or pull forward the panel your extractor is ready for use. When you have finished cooking you close it up and it then sits flush with the adjacent units and totally out of sight.

A canopy extractor is, as the name suggests, designed to sit inside an overhead canopy. Canopies can be made successfully to suit yourself, on site in the kitchen at the time of fitting. Very often they are made up of chipboard, painted and tiled and incorporate wooden or painted cornice as decoration to match the rest of the kitchen.

Copper canopies are also available. I have also seen canopies done in brickwork. Only the more sophisticated rigid kitchen ranges provide a ready-made canopy to suit a canopy extractor and these are usually merely shaped veneer sheeting, and not worth the price which you will be expected to pay for them.

Extractors may be placed on an outside wall in your kitchen and vented out through the wall with a simple venting kit; or they may be positioned anywhere in the room and use disposable charcoal filters, which filter and re-circulate the bad air. Venting is really the most efficient method, but the re-circulation method does work provided you change the charcoal filters regularly, every six to twelve months. Therefore if you use the recirculating method, make sure that you also buy spare sets of the disposable charcoal filters; manufacturers regularly change the types of models available. In other words, if you have an outside wall in the kitchen, try to place the hob and hood on that wall and vent out. If you can't do that then buy a major manufacturer's standard type hood and stock up with spare filters. Most major manufacturers guarantee to provide a spare parts service for extractor fans for ten years, so again it makes sense to buy from a well known company.

Fig 3.15

Fig 3.16

Fig 3.17

Fig 3.15 Basic extractor fan

Fig 3.16 Slimline telescopic fan

Fig 3.17 Canopy extractor

Fridges and freezers

Just as ovens can be built in or under, so can fridges and freezers. Whether you use built-under or built-in fridges and freezers will depend upon what your personal requirements are and how big or small your kitchen is.

Fridges and freezers that are designed to be built in or under may have the facility for a décor panel or an integrated panel, both of which will match your kitchen units. (This also applies to washing machines and dishwashers.)

Décor panel appliances have a little metal trim all the way around the doors of the appliance into which you can slot a 3 mm thick flat veneer panel to match the units. This is the most economical way of achieving that 'hidden' or 'built-in' look in your kitchen.

Integrated doors on your appliances are slightly more sophisticated. This is where an actual solid unit door is attached to the door of the appliance.

Built-in fridges and freezers have to be housed in tall units, just as ovens do. Here too, check your measurements and be sure that the appliance size will suit the aperture of the housing unit.

Built-under fridges and freezers, on the other hand, do not need units, and merely sit in an allotted space under the worktop; they are 'packed up' to the correct height and the plinth runs across the bottom to finish off the 'fitted' look.

Dishwashers and washing machines

Dishwashers and washing machines do not require a housing unit and are treated in the same way as built-under fridges and freezers. One important point when choosing a dishwasher or washing machine is that you must not let the fact that they are built under colour your judgement when it comes to specifications. Some consumers will accept any old machine as long as it gives a co-ordinated look to their kitchen. Refer to manufacturer's fact sheets and check features such as capacity, and generally make sure that the machine itself will be suitable for your purposes before you buy.

Very few manufacturers make a built-in tumble dryer and therefore the inclusion of an oddly sized dryer in your kitchen can spoil the total effect. One answer is to buy a combined washer/tumble dryer for building under, but bear in mind that you won't be able to wash and dry at the same time. Be practical too, and remember that tumble dryers create a lot of condensation; they should be vented outside if indoors, and are very much at home in the carport or garage, particularly if they are only used occasionally. It is worth noting that one of the leading manufacturers is making a smaller built-in tumble dryer that can fit under a sink or be used in a housing unit. Another of their innovative ideas is a smaller dishwasher, which will fit under a sink or in a housing unit. If you have a lack-of-space problem, consider one of these. Refer to the manufacturer for accurate sizes when you are planning them in. In a larger kitchen, you could install two built-in dishwashers, one above the other, one holding clean dishes and one being filled up with dirty ones, and use them alternately. This means you'll always have clean crockery available and you will save a bit on storage space for crockery, too.

Your budget may dictate that you need to incorporate a regular free-standing washing machine. They nearly all use a 600 mm space whether free-standing or built-in. A word of advice when considering free-standing washing machines, however. Do not attempt to incorporate a top-loader since you cannot put a worktop over it, and the same will apply to front-loaders with soap dispensers on the top rather than at the front. Stick to front-loading models that can be built in as easily as purpose-designed built-in ones.

If you are one of the diehards who are still using a twintub washing machine, then it is perfectly possible to adapt a 1000 mm base unit as a 'stowaway' to put your twin tub in and then merely roll it out for use.

Other considerations

There is a lot you can do with regard to space in a small kitchen if you enlist the help of a good carpenter or are handy yourself. For one example, a built-in single oven can be place in a housing unit above a built-under fridge, in instances where space is really tight. Don't worry about the effects of heat, as all good built-in appliances should be adequately vented in the correct manner to emit heat and steam at the front.

Other free-standing appliances can be incorporated in your kitchen. Little inexpensive free-standing fridges are nearly all less than 600 mm wide, but do check the height as they may not sit under a worktop.

You must remember to try not to mix décor panel varieties of appliances with the integrated-door type in your kitchen, or you will end up with a hotch-potch. A further point on this theme is that matching up to achieve a totally fitted look should be very carefully done. Do check that all your appliances co-ordinate colour-wise, and decide on a scheme of things when it comes to the colour of appliances, because you won't want a brown oven, a darker brown hob, a white extractor fan and a stainless steel sinktop, to cite a very obvious example. Remember that you are striving for an overall co-ordinated look, and don't forget matching control panels for your dishwasher or washing machine.

I have, in my time, come across instances of householders going to ridiculous lengths to achieve a built-in look without spending too much money. I have seen sheets of veneer literally superglued to fridges with the raw edges showing in all their glory. I have seen washing machines sprayed with car paint in a none-too-satisfactory manner. Do not go too mad to achieve the built-in look on the cheap.

You would be surprised how nice your fitted kitchen can look with just a well-thought-out run of units and your old appliances to keep you ticking over. If the appliances are properly positioned for functional considerations they shouldn't detract from the overall effect. Even unwieldy tall fridge-freezers, provided they are on the end of a run of units, do not look amiss. Bear in mind, above all, that the kitchen is a workplace and that if it is planned as such will ultimately be pleasant to look at.

Finally, when considering any appliance, check when you buy about guarantees and service facilities. Check that there is an adequate back-up service and that a qualified engineer is only a quick phone call away should your appliance malfunction. Established companies usually have excellent call-out and back-up facilities. Again, this points to the wisdom of buying brand names, buying wisely and buying British.

Check-lists: what to look for when buying appliances

Oven features	Built-in	Built-under	Slot-in
Single or double oven?	Either	Single	Either
Gas or electricity?	Either	Either	Either
Type of housing?	Housing unit or brickwork	Built-under housing unit	None needed
Standard or odd size?	Mostly standard	Standard	Varies
Special housing needed?	For single or odd sizes	Readily available	No
Fan oven available?	Yes	Yes	No
Hob separate or integral?	Separate	Either	Either
Separate grill?	Yes	No	Yes
Space needed?	Minimum 1500 mm	Minimum 600 mm	Minimum 500 mm
Projection-free hob possible?	No	Yes	Yes
Other features?			May have lift-up lid

Fridges and freezers
Fridge-freezer or separate fridge and freezer?

Built-in, built under or slot-in?

Pull-out if built-under?

Side-by-side or one on top of the other, if built-in?

If free-standing, will it fit?

Plinth available if necessary to pack up built-under appliance?

Décor panel?

Integrated door?

Fig 3.18

Fig 3.19

Fig 3.20

Fig 3.18 Built-in fridge and freezer

Fig 3.19 Washing machine with décor panel door

Fig 3.20 Dishwasher with integrated door

Fig 3.21 Built-in fridges and freezers can also be planned in side by side.

Fig 3.22 Built-under fridge and freezer

Fig 3.21

Fig 3.22

SINKTOPS AND TAPS

Your sinktop is a very important consideration, because it is at work at the sink that you will spend the major part of your time in the kitchen. Research has shown that 75 per cent of our time in the kitchen is in fact spent at the sink. The sinktop is also, together with the oven and hob, a major focal point of your kitchen from an aesthetic point of view.

Fig 4.1 Stainless steel sinks are easy to clean

Fig 4.2 Composite sinks are available in a huge variety of styles and colours

Just a few generations ago, with the advent of plumbed-in running water in domestic dwellings, sinktops were large, simple, rectangular affairs of clay material, and this was where the vegetables were prepared, the plates washed up, the babies bathed, the clothes-washing done, and where the adults of the household had their daily strip wash. These simple sinks soon grew wooden draining boards and some even sported a curtain draped around the bottom to achieve a space underneath where cooking utensils could be stored.

It was not until after the Second World War that one-piece sinks and drainers began to appear; and then the curtain gave way to a cupboard. So the sink base unit developed, with a 'sit-on' sink top in either enamelled or stainless steel, or the more traditional ceramic material. By the 1940s, more cupboards had been added and eventually this gave rise to the development of the modern fitted kitchen. By now a larger variety of styles of sinks were available, as sinks had sprouted extra bowls or extra draining boards.

The traditional sink base unit with a 'sit-on' stainless steel sink is still widely available today. There are diehards who still insist on one and smaller builders will frequently use them to cut corners on building costs, but there is no doubt that the modern inset type of sinktop is an improvement on its forerunners.

With the development of waterproof mastic and clamps and bolts to hold the sink in position it became possible to cut out worktops and seal 'inset' sinks into the surface of the top, and it is the inset type of sink that is generally planned into a fitted kitchen today.

Inset sinks are, by design, hygienic, because it is easy to keep the surrounding area of the sinktop clean. They also look neat and tidy, and are a boon when planning a kitchen because they take up relatively less space than their forerunners. For example, an inset sinktop will sit nicely in a 600 mm wide base unit, leaving the drainer to lie over a washing machine or dishwasher, whereas even the smallest 'sit-on' type needs a whole 1000 mm base unit to itself.

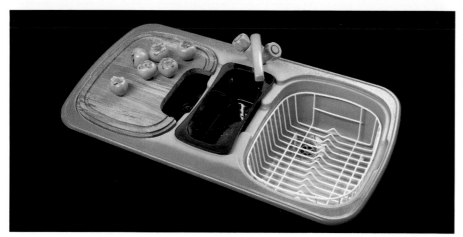

Sink construction materials and finishes

A decade ago, inset sinktops, as well as their sit-on counterparts were either of enamelled or stainless steel, and enamel was very fashionable on account of its being available in a variety of colours. In fact at one point sink manufacturers were making almost nothing else. Enamelled sinks are still generally available nowadays. They are made from mild steel coated with tough enamel, and because enamel is a type of glaze, i.e. glass, there are still many older kitchens around with scratched and chipped sinks, since the glaze is susceptible to damage if mistreated during transit, installation, or everyday use in the kitchen.

On the other hand, stainless steel as a sink material has continued to prove its worth; stainless sinktops continue to be produced in very modern designs, as well as being still available in the more traditional versions. Stainless steel has a nickel and chromium content and a good stainless steel sink should be made from 18/8 material, which stands for 18 per cent chromium and 8 per cent nickel. Some continental manufacturers use 18/10 or 18/12 stainless steel, because the extra nickel content makes the material softer and easier to shape. However, in this country it is generally accepted that 18/8 gives the best finish and hardest surface.

The actual steel sheet itself should be between 0.7 and 0.9 mm thick. Some manufacturers, whether continental or British, use a thinner steel sheet and therefore, here again, ask relevant questions of the salesperson, read the brochures carefully, buy good brand names, and try to buy British. There is another consideration: it is still possible to come across very cheap steel sinks which are formed in the same way as the ones previously described, but from steel called 'ferritic' (as opposed to 'austenitic') because it has been formed at a lower temperature (up to about 1350°F). Ferritic steel is magnetic and can rust. If you decide upon a stainless steel sinktop, only buy a good quality 'austenitic' steel one. Austenitic stainless steel cannot rust. If rust spots do appear, they will have been caused by the use of wire wool, or by water-borne particles which have adhered to the sinktop. Therefore, when you buy your stainless steel sink, throw out those wire wool cleaning pads, and if you do eventually have a problem with rust spots, consult either the manufacturer or a good plumber. Generally speaking, stainless steel will not stain, but certain concentrated household chemicals, such as bleach, sterilising solution, photographic chemicals and metal dips, can cause corrosion and discolouration if allowed to remain on the surface. The keynote is, whatever you use in the kitchen, keep your sink clean at all times.

During the last decade, 'composite' sinks have become increasingly popular and are at present showing increasingly significant sales figures in the sinktop market as a whole. Where the composite sink material was actually developed is unsure, but in the early 1970s ICI developed a material known as 'asterite', which is now only one of the vast array of composite sink materials available in the United Kingdom and manufactured both here and on the continent. The United Kingdom is, in fact, very much the heart of composite sink manufacture.

Fig 4.3 The traditional 'sit on' sinktop

Fig 4.4 The new style of sink is inset into the worktop

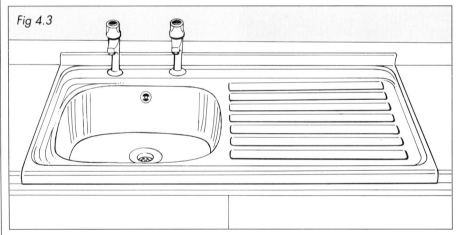

Fig 4.3

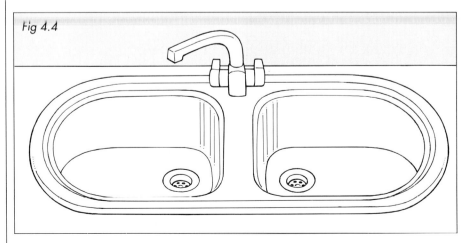

Fig 4.4

Composite sinks are made by binding silica particles in a variety of acrylic or epoxy compounds. There are all sorts of variations on this theme using slightly different proportions of materials and chemicals, and different methods of casting and heating. There are at present, to my knowledge, twenty-one manufacturers of composite sinktops, using eight different materials selling under thirteen different brand names, namely:

resilica; starflex; silacron; silquartz; sylac; carbonite; astron; fradura; velstra; decopland; resan; reston; and teka.

Looking at just one of these at random – silquartz – we discover that the manufacturers claim that it has an impact-, scratch-, stain- and temperature resistance higher than sinks made from either stainless or enamelled steel. They maintain that you can drop a 2 kg pan on it from a height of one metre without denting, chipping, scratching or marking the surface of the sink in any way. They add that the surface of the sink will withstand temperatures of up to 230°C and that, all in all, silquartz sinks will withstand forces that would damage enamelled steel or dent stainless steel.

In the last seven years the complaints I have encountered about composite sinks have been with regard to their cleanability. They are more difficult to keep clean than stainless steel sinks, and limescale can sometimes result in a more permanent discolouration problem. Again, as with stainless steel sinks, the keynote is constant cleanliness.

Popular at present with the increasing vogue for 'Victoriana' are brass inset sinktops, and very often these are two circular inset bowls, although other better styles are available. I remain unconvinced that brass is an intelligent choice of material, on account of its tending to deteriorate with age and also its cleanability. You'll have to use brass polish now and again.

Recently there has been a growing demand for deeper bowls, although for many years now modern sinks have tended to be shallow. A few enlightened manufacturers are selling deep bowls in modern configurations and materials, and some purchasers are reverting to the old-fashioned rectangular fireclay sink and incorporating it into a modern kitchen. This type is called a 'Belfast' sink and will be available from more traditional builders' merchants; but it is only available in white, and you will need to pay particular attention to how you plan it in, since modern units aren't designed to cope with it.

Incidentally, there are just a few sanitaryware manufacturers who do produce modern sinktops in traditional fireclay, but these tend to be costly.

On the whole, composite sinks and good quality stainless steel sinks carry comparable prices; enamel can usually be bought quite cheaply; and brass and fireclay are more expensive.

Configurations of bowls and drainers

In general, manufacturers are now more adventurous and thoughtful in terms of the design of their sinktops.

Nowadays there are a variety of exciting designs and they are almost as various as the types of kitchen units.

Fig 4.5

Fig 4.6

Fig 4.7

Fig 4.5 Single bowl and single drainer

Fig 4.6 Single bowl and double drainer

Fig 4.7 2¹/₂ bowl and single drainer

Fig 4.8 1¹/₂ bowl and single drainer

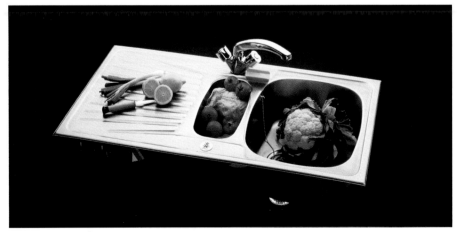

Fig 4.8

Modern sinks often have a 'pop-up' waste. These are useful because they are operated by a nob on the top of the sink, so you don't need to get your hands wet when emptying the sink. This avoids the recurrent problem of the plug coming off the chain and of scouring shops for a new chain when the original goes missing.

Fig 4.9

Fig 4.10

Fig 4.11

Fig 4.9 Two circular inset bowls with mono-mixer tap

Fig 4.10 Two circular bowls and a mono-mixer tap can be inset into a worktop.

Fig 4.11 Some manufacturers now make sinks with larger or deeper bowls than usual

Fig 4.12 Sink with 'pop-up' waste

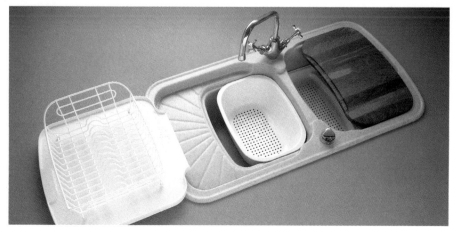

Fig 4.12

Fig 4.13 1³/₄ bowl and drainer

Fig 4.14 2¹/₂ bowl

Fig 4.15 1¹/₂ bowl and double drainer

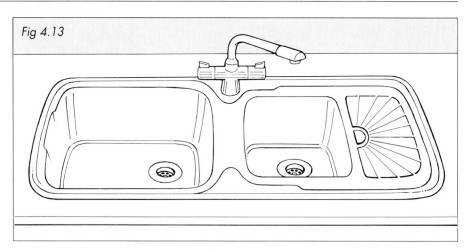

Fig 4.13

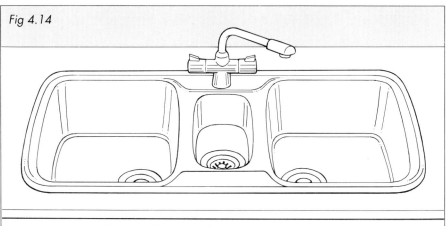

Fig 4.14

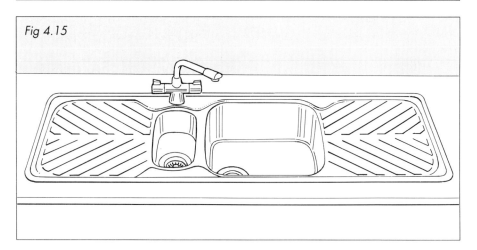

Fig 4.15

Accessories and wastes

Modern sinktops tend to come with sets of accessories which are very useful. The most common combination of accessories is a basket for draining crockery; a strainer bowl for vegetable peeling, rinsing, straining and defrosting; and a chopping board for preparing meat, fish and vegetables. Washing-up liquid dispensers may also be available.

Consider the usefulness of some, any, or all of these accessories and consider too their durability and the colours in which they are available; make sure you don't upset the total colour scheme of your kitchen. A good tip when buying accessories is to buy two sets, i.e., a spare set for future use, because they won't generally last the time of the sinktop, and each make and style of sink requires different sizes and shapes of accessories.

When purchasing a sinktop, verify that the accessories are included in the price of the sink rather than extra to it. You can also ask if the price includes the wastes too: very often it doesn't. To my mind, a well-thought-out package is one where the sink price includes a complete set of accessories and all the wastes required.

Incidentally, whilst on the subject of sink wastes: a standard kitchen waste is usually designed to fit a 38 mm waste outlet, unless the sinktop is imported. Many modern sinks also have in the smaller bowl an 89 mm size waste outlet designed to take either a 'basket strainer waste' – a large waste incorporating a removable straining part which catches peelings and food scraps – or a waste disposal unit.

If you want a waste disposal unit check that you have the correct size outlet on your sink. In fact, do check in general that you will be able to purchase, whether separately or complete, the correct wastes for the sinktop of your choice. Should you decide that you would prefer to use the larger waste on your sink for a waste disposal unit, refer to page 43.

Fig 4.16 Basket strainer waste

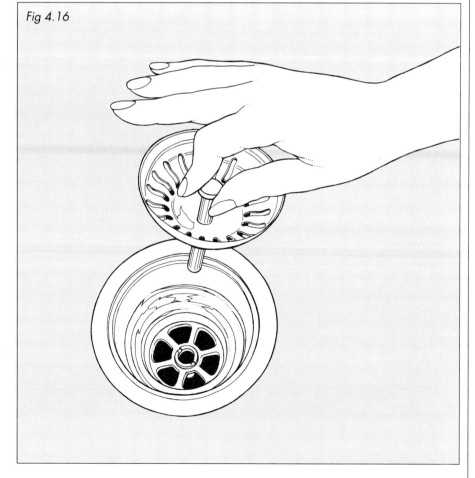

Fig 4.16

What do you need from a sink?

When you are considering purchasing a sinktop you should analyse your own requirements from a variety of angles. You must give thought to its durability; its practicality; and to its aesthetic appeal; and usually in that order of priorities.

First decide on the type of material you would prefer, and then decide on the combination of bowls and drainers that you will need. You may require only a single bowl or a double drainer sink and so on. The next step is to decide if the configuration of sink you would prefer will in fact be practicable in relation to the size of your kitchen. In a very small kitchen you may need to limit yourself to the smallest single bowl and single drainer. If you have oceans of space then you could go as far as a double bowl, double drainer for example. The acid test of this will of course come at the planning stage - so try in the first instance to keep your options relatively open and keep a variety of configurations in mind.

Finally, look at the style of the sink. Is it pleasant to the eye? Is it well designed? For example, will the water running from the draining board run straight back into the bowl you are washing the strawberries in, or is there an outlet to prevent this? Is there a good raised rim all around the sink to avoid continually wetting the worktop? These are just some of the many questions you should ask yourself after you have considered which functions you yourself usually perform at your sinktop.

Fig 4.17 Sink pillar-taps

Fig 4.18 Deck sink-mixer-taps, Monobloc sink-mixer-taps, and Deck sink mixer with swan neck

Taps

We have ascertained that when purchasing a sink we need to be clear about buying it complete with all necessary accessories and wastes. Your tap, on the other hand, will be a separate item since you want to give as much careful thought to your choice of tap as you have given to your sinktop.

You will have noticed in the preceding section that some sinktops have two tapholes whereas some have only one. It is also a fact that many composite sinks have no tapholes at all; the taphole is punched out in situ on either the front or the back of the sink, thus making it multi-handed; i.e. a left-hand or a right-hand drainer, depending on which way round the unit is fitted. Some sinktops have no tapholes and cannot be punched and with these the tap itself is set into the worktop.

The first and most obvious point to consider is that you must choose a tap suitable for your sinktop. Basically there are three styles of taps: sink pillar-taps; deck sink-mixer-taps; and monobloc sink-mixer-taps. The first two styles suit a sinktop with two tapholes and the latter is for use on sinktops with either one or no tapholes.

Fig 4.19 Sinks with two tapholes can be fitted to be either left- of right-handed

Fig 4.20 Lever handles are available on various tap styles, and are helpful for elderly or disabled people.

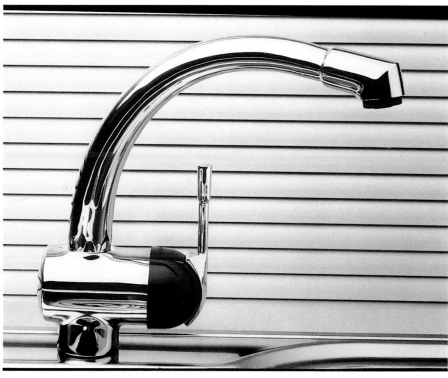

Sink pillar-taps

There are a multitude of variations within these three basic styles. Traditional hot and cold brass sink pillar-taps have cross heads; they may be very basic and just like grandma used, or a rather posh copy - in polished brass or gold with porcelain indices - of taps like those Queen Victoria might have used. Obviously the former will cost you pennies and the latter will cost you many pounds,

Modern hot and cold sink pillar-taps are mainly of chrome on brass and have either perspex or chrome-plated heads. Try to go for a chrome-plated head, as perspex tends to crack and discolour with time; but ensure too that you are not just buying chrome-plated plastic heads, but actual metal heads. Whatever head you choose, check that it is easy to turn.

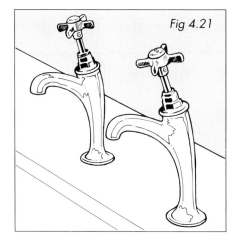

Fig 4.21

Lever-operated single pillar-taps are also available, and these are good for the elderly, infirm and arthritic.

With the revival of the traditional Belfast fireclay sinktop, certain interest has also been aroused in the wall mounted 'bib' tap.

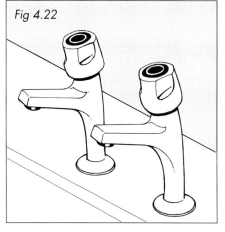

Fig 4.22

Fig 4.24

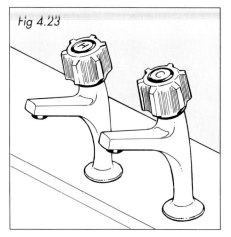

Fig 4.23

Fig 4.21 'Victoriana' sink pillar-taps

Fig 4.22 Chrome-plated heads on sink pillar taps

Fig 4.23 Perspex heads on sink pillar taps

Fig 4.24 'Bib' taps on Belfast sink

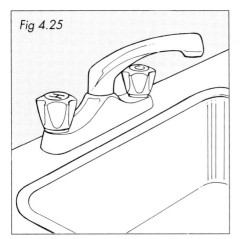

Fig 4.25

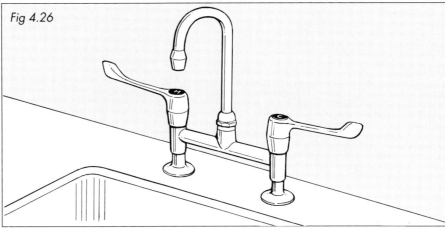

Fig 4.26

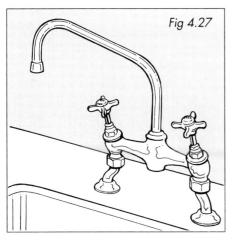

Fig 4.27

Deck sink-mixer-taps

The same principles apply when buying a deck sink-mixer-tap as when buying single hot and cold pillar taps. All deck mixers should have swivel spouts, but do also consider the size, height and reach of the spout too.

Consider, too, the filling of buckets at the kitchen sink. Can you stand a bucket easily underneath the tap, for instance? Can you use a hosepipe on the tap? Can you wash the kids' hair underneath the tap?

Deck sink-mixer-taps are also available with lever handles, and, again, reproduction styles are now available.

Fig 4.25 Standard deck sink-mixer

Fig 4.26 Deck sink-mixer with lever handles

Fig 4.27 'Victoriana' deck sink-mixer

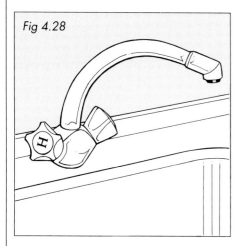

Fig 4.28

Monobloc sink-mixer-taps

We must apply the same principles when choosing a monobloc sink-mixer-tap. Check the handles and spout. There are several types available: monobloc sink-mixers with lever handles, and monobloc sink-mixers with a single lever 'joystick', as well as the more usual style of handles. Some manufacturers make a 'swan-neck' mixer tap, which is particularly good for a $1^1/2$ sinktop, because the spout swivels out over the large bowl. There is also the quarter-turn ceramic disc-action mixer

Ceramic disc-action taps

Ceramic disc-action taps are becoming increasingly popular, both in the kitchen and the bathroom. Conventionally, the flow of water from a tap is controlled by a valve and a washer. All of us must have had some experience of having to replace tap washers from time to time! On a ceramic disc-action tap, the valve and washer are replaced by a cartridge, inside which there are ceramic discs. Manufacturers have claimed, since the invention of these discs a few years ago, that the discs are immune to corrosion and will last for almost a lifetime, whilst at the same time reducing the possibility of leaks or drips.

However, all tap manufacturers producing ceramic disc-action taps have experienced problems. Complaints from customers have varied from those who found they had hardly any water coming through the tap to those who had a constant deluge which could not be stopped. Others have had handles stiffen and seize up.

My own experience and that of many plumbers indicates that these problems occur because ceramic discs are really only suitable for a 'tank fed' water supply. (Note well that most kitchen cold water supply is from the mains and since we tend to take our drinking water from the kitchen, this is the sensible arrangement.) Manufacturers that I have approached with this anomaly have merely reassured me that they are perfecting and improving the design of their ceramic disc-action taps all the time and they should be suitable for mains water.

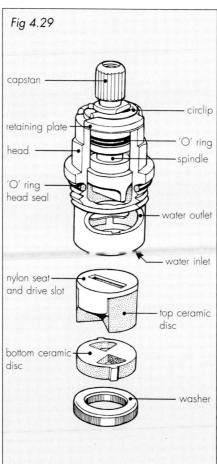

Fig 4.29

capstan

circlip

retaining plate

'O' ring

head

spindle

'O' ring head seal

water outlet

water inlet

nylon seat and drive slot

top ceramic disc

bottom ceramic disc

washer

I have ceramic disc-action taps throughout my house. The taps in the bathroom are fine; the tap in the kitchen has constantly had to have cartridges replaced and never performs well. I will leave you to draw your own conclusions.

Materials and colours

The style, look and feel of your tap are also to be taken into consideration, and will be dictated by the materials of which the tap is made and finished. A lot of taps are made with a body of brass. 'Brass-finished' taps are then generally lacquered. 'Chrome-finished' taps are chromium plate on brass. Coloured taps are either nylon- or enamel-finished.

The usual combinations are chrome-plated taps on a stainless steel sinktop and coloured nylon- or enamel-finished taps on a composite or enamel coloured sinktop.

You can of course vary these general themes, bearing in mind the general colour scheme in your kitchen. There is nothing to prevent you putting a smart cherry-red mixer tap on a white composite sink and matching it up to bright red accessories, for example.

As the demand for coloured composite sinks has increased, so has the demand for matching mixer taps. The most popular colours here are beiges and browns, and there are so many shades of both taps and sinks available that unless you specify that you require the same manufacturer to supply the sinktop and matching taps that have been specially manufactured to co-ordinate, you may find yourself with a nasty mismatch of shades.

Whichever type and style of tap you choose, again, try to buy British. Foreign taps come in two varieties; the very cheap and nasty and the ultra-modern and expensive. Certainly your tap should conform to British Standard BS5412/3, 1976 which ensures that it has been tested to ascertain an adequate flow rate. With regard to local water by-laws, which concern themselves with water wastage and the prevention of contamination of water supplies, you will need to consult a good plumber.

Fig 4.30

Accessories

Finally, there are a variety of accessories available with certain makes of taps. You can have a rinse attachment with a brush and so on. Always remember that accessories such as these may seem attractive and may indeed prove useful, but that their lifespan will in no way match up to that of the sinktop or tap, and that sooner or later they will need to be replaced. Usually such things need to be replaced as soon as they are no longer available!

In brief then:
a) Ensure your tap fits your sink taphole system
b) Ensure your tap is of a good quality throughout
c) Ensure your tap meets your individual requirements
d) Ensure your tap is colour co-ordinated to both your sinktop and your scheme in the kitchen in general.

Above all be decisive, because at the last count there were just over 40 different brands of taps available in Britain!

Checklists: what to look for when buying sinks and taps

Sinktops	Taps
Inset or sit-on?	Style of tap?
Enamel, stainless steel or composite?	Style of tap suitable for sink?
Quality of stainless steel?	Chrome or brass-plated heads if sink-pillar-taps?
Number of sinks?	Lever-operated?
Number of drainers?	Size, height and reach of spout if deck sink mixer tap?
Deep bowl available?	Ceramic disc action?
Desired accessories available?	Brass, chrome or nylon or enamel-finished body?
Accessories included in price?	Matching to sinks OK?
Correct wastes available?	Accessories available?
Wastes included in price?	Accessories included in price?
Basket strainer waste or waste disposal facility?	
Well designed sink?	

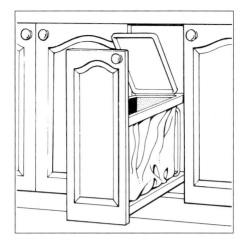

Waste disposal units and waste disposal systems

In the section about sinktops we touched upon the subject of waste disposal units to be incorporated into your sinktop; the disposal of kitchen waste in general is worth some discussion.

Originally we threw our kitchen rubbish out of the window or over the wall. With technological growth, an increase in population, and an increase in waste in general we became aware of the need for an organised system of disposal, and the advent of plastics popularised the kitchen waste bin, which many still solely rely upon today.

We inherited waste disposal units from the Americans approximately twenty years ago, and more than two-thirds of the world's waste disposal units are still made in the United States. Research has shown that only about 10 per cent of people fitting a new kitchen in the United Kingdom opt for a waste disposal unit; but it also shows that over 90 per cent of these people would buy another if their machine broke down or died of old age; or if they moved home.

Waste disposal units take material consisting mainly of food waste, grind it into a slurry, and with the addition of cold water whilst the disposer is being electrically operated, dispose of the slurry by washing it away into the drainage system.

Before you rush to buy such a useful toy, consider what kitchen rubbish you actually accumulate. Remember that the major part of kitchen rubbish in the 1980s (and undoubtedly through the 1990s) will be paper and plastic packaging, which cannot be put in a waste disposal unit. Neither can tin cans or other containers.

Also mull over factors such as pets you have who may eat food scraps, or if you are a keen gardener, having a compost heap. Certainly the trend in eating habits in the 80s is for ready-prepared food in packaging and thus less actual food waste is created than in the good old days when Mum always shopped locally and nearly always prepared 'meat and two veg'.

If, however, you do feel the need for a waste disposal, then consider that there are two types generally available, both fitting neatly under the sink and powered by electricity.

The continuous-feed waste disposal unit has an on - off switch mounted away from the disposal unit itself. Once the switch is turned on you can continuously feed waste into the machine whilst the cold tap runs. Most models have some type of reversing system in case the machine jams, and also a perforated shield to put over the neck of the machine, to prevent items such as cutlery accidentally falling in.

The batch-feed waste disposal unit generally switches on automatically when you load it with waste and water and turn the neck. When it has disposed of this first load you may then reload and so on. This means that it works with a lid on, unlike the continuous-feed system, and this is a very important safety consideration.

Also available in today's market place are rubbish compactors: these are free-standing cabinets to be placed in the kitchen, and are electrically operated. They compress rubbish to 25 per cent of its original volume with a force of about $2^{1}/_{2}$ tonnes.

Other innovations include having a section of the sinktop that opens directly into a chute, with a bin stored underneath; and cut-outs in the worktop which use the same system. There is now even a chute system, in which you cut a hole in your wall, seal it with a magnetic door, and feed your rubbish directly outside to your dustbin.

The majority of kitchen unit manufacturers provide waste bins; these can be either the simple back-door style in stainless steel or plastic, or a more sophisticated pull-out style, in which case the bin takes up a whole kitchen unit and automatically pulls out and opens when you open the unit door.

All kitchens require some system of rubbish and waste disposal and with thought, the plastic carrier bag hanging off the handle of a cupboard and spilling nasty rubbish can be easily eliminated!

RANGES OF UNITS AVAILABLE

It is wise, before planning, to familiarise yourself to some extent with the basic range of units that are readily available on the market. I have, in preceding chapters already spoken about the difference between self-assembly and rigid ranges. I will here concentrate on familiarising you with a typical basic self-assembly range, since they are by far the most popular.

Having read this chapter, procure a manufacturer's price list from the kitchen supplier of your choice, which will outline and illustrate in full the entire choice of different units available in that particular range, and give measurements and prices.

You will find that with rigid kitchens the choice is almost limitless and that with self-assembly ranges the choice is limited but still adequate. After considering price lists you may then be led to prefer one range above another, reject another outright, and so on. Don't make this decision just on a financial basis either; but make sure that the manufacturer does supply the particular units you would like.

In general, heights of units may vary fractionally from one manufacturer's range to another, but widths are all standard, and nowadays always metric. Almost all kitchens are 600 mm deep, so standard built-in appliances can be easily incorporated.

So as not to be confused by all the different sizes, in the first instance the amateur kitchen planner need only concern her or himself with the width of the unit. It is in fact the width that is all important and thus when one refers to a 300 mm base unit, it is, in fact, the width that dictates the name of the unit. The following illustrations will show common units that are available in most manufacturers' ranges and which, in combination, are more than adequate to plan a complete fitted kitchen.

All of these units will have option of being 'drawerline' or 'doorline'. Drawerline units have a drawer at the top of each unit and therefore every base unit in your kitchen will have a drawer at the top.

'Doorline' units have a full-height door and no drawer and consequently, somewhere in your kitchen you must incorporate a 'drawerpack', which is usually 500 mm wide.

Whether you prefer the drawerline look and arrangement or the doorline style is a matter of personal choice, but I myself would opt for doorline on the following grounds:

a) There is less bending to get access into the unit.

b) There is more storage space for large packets and tall bottles in a doorline unit.

c) Having drawers scattered all round the kitchen, is to my mind, less efficient.

d) Because a doorline unit is a simpler construction, a doorline kitchen costs proportionally less than its drawerline equivalent.

Fig 5.1   Fig 5.2

Fig 5.1 Doorline kitchen

Fig 5.2 Drawerline kitchen

Base units

Fig 5.3 300 mm base unit

Fig 5.4 500 mm base unit

Fig 5.5 600 mm base unit

Fig 5.6 1000 mm base unit

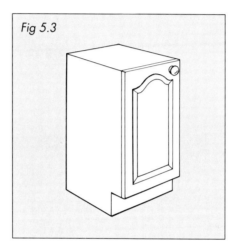

Fig 5.3

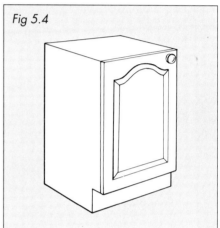

Fig 5.4

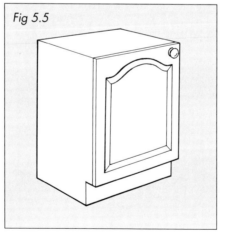

Fig 5.5

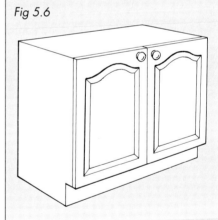

Fig 5.6

Tall units

Fig 5.7

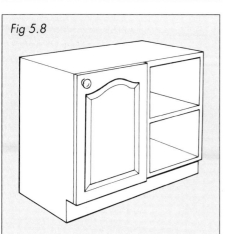

Fig 5.8

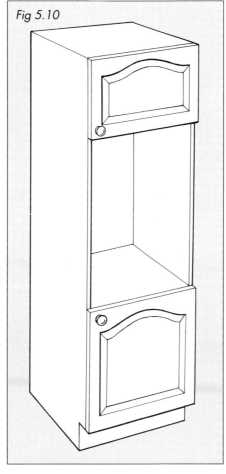

Fig 5.10

Fig 5.11

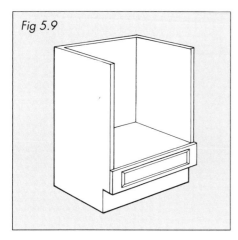

Fig 5.9

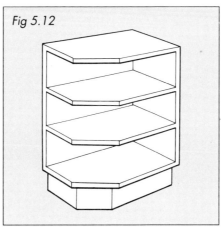

Fig 5.12

Fig 5.7 500 mm drawer pack

Fig 5.8 1000 mm corner base unit. Note that this unit physically occupies 1100 mm of space.

Fig 5.9 600 mm built-under oven single housing

Fig 5.10 600 mm tall double oven housing unit

Fig 5.11 500 mm broom / larder unit

Fig 5.12 800 mm base open-end shelves

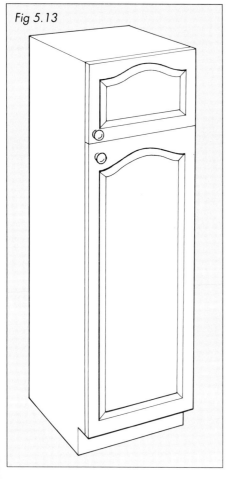

Fig 5.13

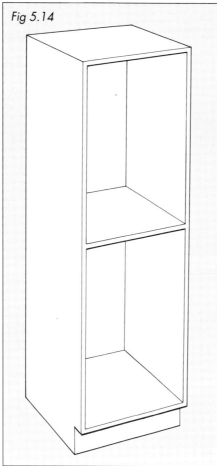

Fig 5.14

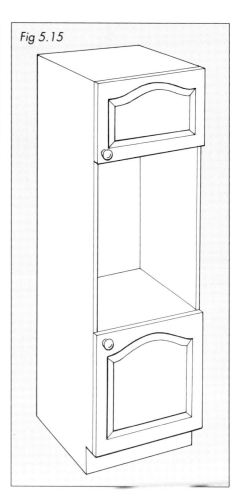

Fig 5.15

Fig 5.13 600 mm broom / larder unit

Fig 5.14 600 mm fridge and freezer housing

Fig 5.15 600 mm fridge-freezer housing

Wall units

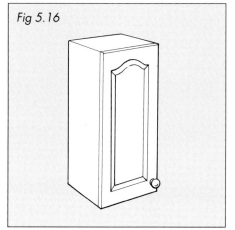

Fig 5.16

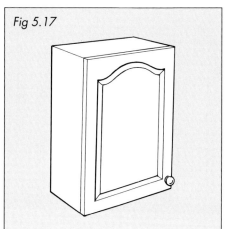

Fig 5.17

Fig 5.16 300 mm standard wall unit
Fig 5.17 500 mm standard wall unit
Fig 5.18 600 mm standard wall unit
Fig 5.19 1000 mm standard wall unit
Fig 5.20 500 mm glass wall unit
Fig 5.21 1000 mm glass wall unit

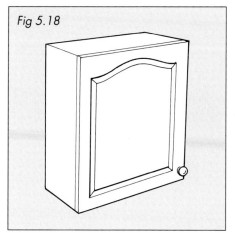

Fig 5.18

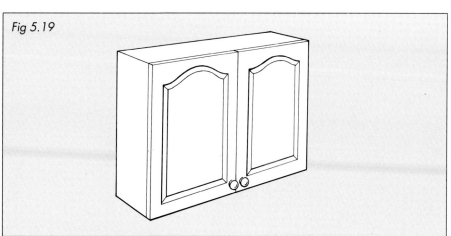

Fig 5.19

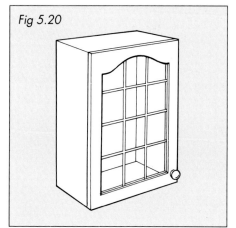

Fig 5.20

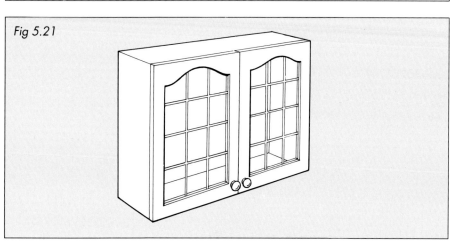

Fig 5.21

Fig 5.24 300 mm open-end wall shelves

Fig 5.25 600 mm cooker hood wall unit

Fig 5.26 500 mm top box

Fig 5.27 600 mm top box

All the above are available as full wall units, where you require taller then standard units. When using these taller versions you must remember two things. First of all you need a 500 mm or 600 mm top box to raise the height of your tall appliances housings or larders correspondingly.

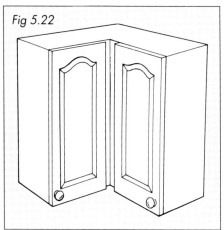

Fig 5.22

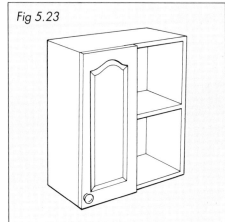

Fig 5.23

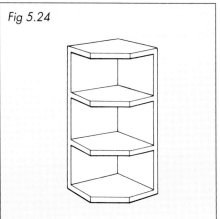

Fig 5.24

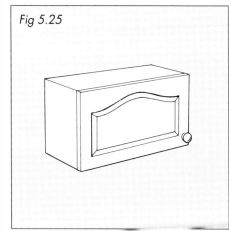

Fig 5.25

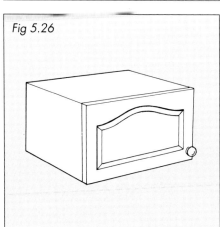

Fig 5.26

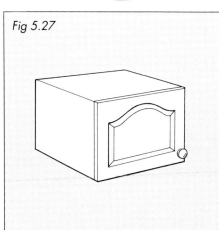

Fig 5.27

Secondly because you are now raising
the total height of the kitchen units, you
may now use a 600 mm standard wall
unit in place of a cooker hood unit, in
most cases. Do check the manufacturer's
literature on this point, because some tall
wall units are not tall enough to warrant
a standard wall unit as a cooker hood
and still require the use of a cooker
hood wall unit.

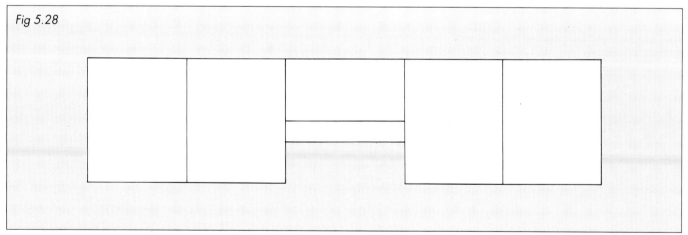

Fig 5.28

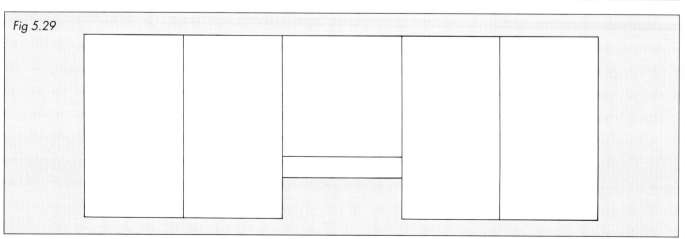

Fig 5.29

Fig 5.30

Sundry items

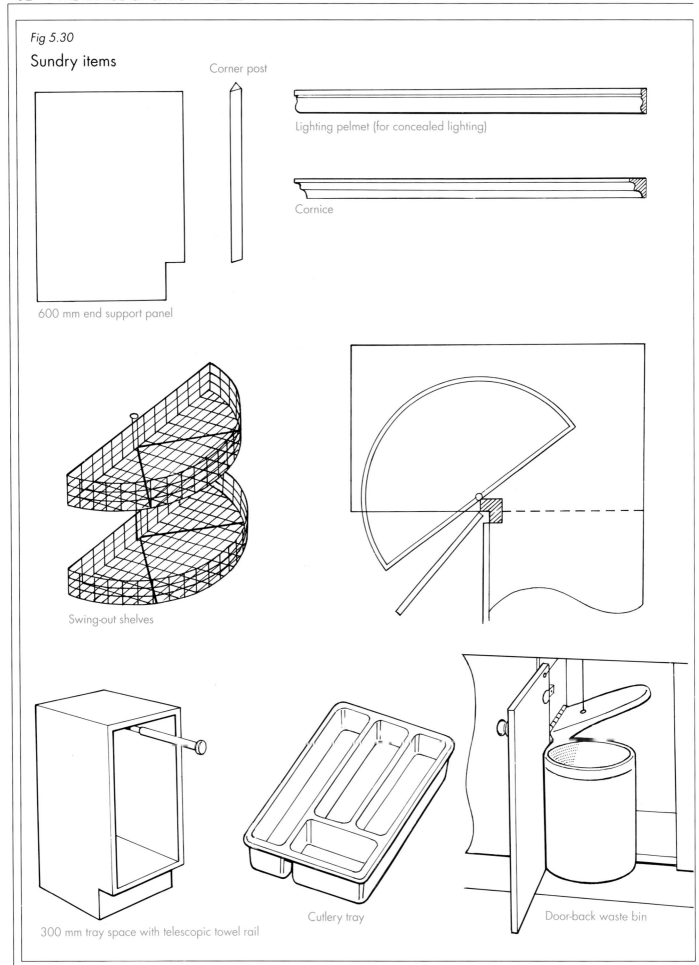

Corner post

Lighting pelmet (for concealed lighting)

Cornice

600 mm end support panel

Swing-out shelves

300 mm tray space with telescopic towel rail

Cutlery tray

Door-back waste bin

Fig 5.31 A good self-assembly kitchen unit range will contain enough items to make the most of most kitchens.

PLANNING YOUR FITTED KITCHEN

Personal considerations

Before you start to measure your kitchen walls it is wise to perform a little questionnaire exercise and do some personal 'market research'. It is as well to do this with the rest of the family, and make notes as you go. In my house I regularly call general family meetings to keep the household running smoothly, and I'd certainly want one when it came to an issue as large, costly and important as a fitted kitchen. Try them! They can be constructive fun for all the family.

The first thing you need to ascertain is the number of people using the kitchen. Then you can make a note of their relative ages and the times at which they are using the kitchen on the whole. For example, in my house, although three people use the kitchen, because they are all getting up at different times, they rarely all use it at the same time. We even do the cooking and washing up on a rota basis. However, this may be atypical and you must determine and consider your own family's lifestyle.

Next, consider any household pets. Where do they eat? Where do they sleep? I once planned a kitchen for an old lady to incorporate sleeping space for five large dogs. Many homes will have pets, and most of these homes will be treating their live-in pets as one of the family too.

Take account next of hobbies. I have one friend whose breakfast bar is a permanent siting for one or more giant jigsaws. Photographic buffs often use the kitchen as a dark room. Amateur wine-makers will undoubtedly require the use of the kitchen. Even hill walkers and gardeners need space for muddy boots, and so on. Consider each member of the family in the light of their leisure activities and with relevance to their use of the kitchen. Particularly where children and teenagers are involved, then consider artistic activities, homework, and entertainment. For example, my cat is housed happily under the breakfast bar whilst my daughter spends hours wrestling with arithmetic above. Smaller children are safer painting in the kitchen than anywhere else in the house. Portable televisions sited on a relevant part of the worktop can provide alternative entertainment while you're peeling the spuds or when grandad is in the lounge watching that one programme that you cannot stand. As a matter of interest, one of last year's kitchen design awards went to the designer who incorporated a built-in television and music centre in his plan.

Consider eating habits carefully. How often do you shop? How much and what type of food do you store? Do you need a large freezer or just a tiny fridge? How much storage space do you require for dry goods? Where will the fresh vegetables go when you've thrown out that wire vegetable rack in the corner to make room for units? One businessman whose conference kitchen I designed specified having a dozen larder units adapted to take crates of wine and beer for use when entertaining. How often and where do you entertain?

Will you profit from the incorporation of a breakfast bar of some description, and how many will it need to seat at once? Would space for a table suit your lifestyle better? Do you slum it in front of the telly with a takeaway or do you give large formal dinner parties?

Make a survey of the number of worktop electrical appliances you use constantly; the consequent worktop space required and the siting of electric sockets. Not only must you take account of your freestanding microwave, but also lesser creatures such as kettles, deep-fat fryers, electric can openers, electric carving knives, food mixers, processors and blenders, and so on. Note which you do possess and which of these are in constant everyday use.

Just as you have considered storage of foodstuffs, consider storage of saucepans and china and glass. You may have a set of copper pans that you wish to display, or you may want to set off cut glass and bone china in a glass-faced unit; and don't forget to take account of your everyday crockery, which has to be adequately housed.

Storage of cleaning materials is just as relevant. These days there are powders, liquids, sprays and aerosols for just about everything. I have one whole base unit devoted to a huge assortment which ranges from heel-renew through ceramic 'hob-shine' liquid to cat-flea spray and ant killer, as well as the more usual cleaners, detergents and disinfectants. On the other hand I have an elderly bachelor relative whose only investment in cleaning materials is a packet of household soda, a tin of wax polish, and a few yellow dusters. Think about what you buy, what you store and what you use, and in what sort of quantities.

Laundry so often gets neglected when it comes to kitchen planning. As I mentioned when we looked at washing machines, the British generally cope with laundry in the kitchen. Do not overlook ironing boards and irons, laundry baskets and drying racks. These items are large and need to be stored. Moreover very often ironing and drying gets done in the kitchen.

Once you have left no stone unturned to uncover your own family's needs and the relevant necessities in terms of features and storage in your kitchen then you can finally discuss styles of doorfronts and colour schemes. For my part, I think that styles and colours are a very personal thing, and if you are looking for ideas there is a wealth of literature, books and magazines, as well as manufacturer's brochures, all available in bookshops, libraries and from many outlets. For some unknown reason this is where your family conference may come to blows if you are of certain temperaments. During my time in kitchen showrooms I have been witness to many almost-divorces on the grounds of disagreement over the colour of a worktop or the style of handles.

Finally, and very important, you must consider your budget. The general consensus of opinion is that you should be quite happy to part with anything up to 10 per cent of the value of your property when refurbishing your kitchen. Estate Agents and Building Societies consider that up to 10 per cent of the value of your property spent on your kitchen can be called an investment, since most of the amount you have spent will be recouped in the increased re-sale value of your house. The experts maintain that, presuming the rest of the house is in good order, then you should recoup 80 per cent of the cost of your kitchen when you sell. They also point out that a good fitted kitchen will always enable you to sell your house more quickly.

The kitchen world also holds that the average person wants to spend £2000 on their kitchen: split into £1500 to be spent on units and appliances, and £500 on fitting. Thus we have an anomaly: unless the vast majority of people live in properties valued at £20,000 we are, generally, underpricing our kitchens.

Whatever you spend on your kitchen - whether you are just smartening it up or considering a total revamp - if you choose wisely then it will be money well spent.

Kitchen layouts

Before you actually start to work on your own kitchen, it is as well to consider the different basic types of layouts; these are used as guidelines or examples when studying the planning of kitchens.

The simplest layout of all is the single-line 'corridor' arrangement with all the appliances and units along one wall only. This layout is fine for very narrow kitchens or small flats.

Fig 6.1 Corridor kitchen

Fig 6.2 Plan of corridor kitchen layout: the 'working triangle' here is a straight line.

Fig 6.1

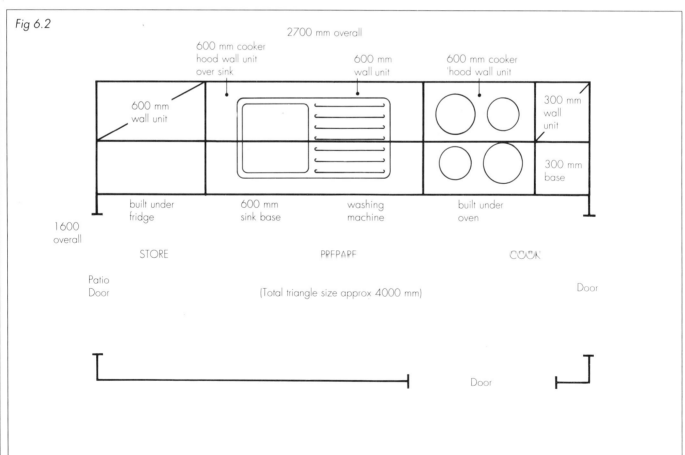

Fig 6.2

2700 mm overall

600 mm cooker hood wall unit over sink

600 mm wall unit

600 mm cooker 'hood wall unit

600 mm wall unit

300 mm wall unit

300 mm base

built under fridge

600 mm sink base

washing machine

built under oven

1600 overall

STORE

PREPARE

COOK

Patio Door

(Total triangle size approx 4000 mm)

Door

Door

Fig 6.3

Fig 6.4

Fig 6.5

Fig 6.3 Galley kitchen layout

Fig 6.4 L-shaped kitchen layout (page 59)

Fig 6.5 U-shaped kitchen layout (page 61)

A continuation of this theme is the 'galley' kitchen. Here the units and appliances are positioned along two facing walls.

If the galley-type kitchen has a door at either end, then the sink and oven and hob should be positioned on the same side, if possible, to eliminate the danger of the cook colliding with 'through traffic'. If there is only one door, it will be possible to site the oven and hob opposite the sink as the distance between the two will be minimal. In a galley kitchen a comfortable working distance between two opposite work surfaces is 1200 mm. This will allow easy access into the units. A distance of 1000 mm is minimal but workable.

Fig 6.6 Plan of galley kitchen: here the oven, hob and sink are on the same side, to minimise the danger of 'through traffic' colliding with the cook.

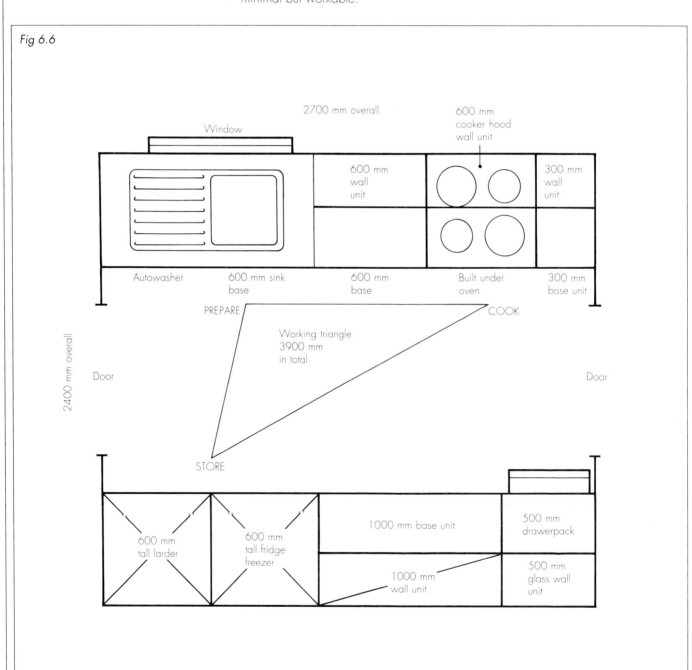

Fig 6.6

The most usual type of kitchen layout is the 'L-shaped' layout. Here units and appliances are laid out on two adjacent walls. In an average sized kitchen and for a family of average requirements, an L-shaped kitchen can easily incorporate all the necessary appliances and features. With modern corner units using swing shelves or corner carousels it is even possible to make good use of that previously cluttered and forgotten corner. The L-shaped layout also allows traffic flow to pass without interruption in the working area.

Fig 6.7 Plan of L-shaped kitchen

Fig 6.7

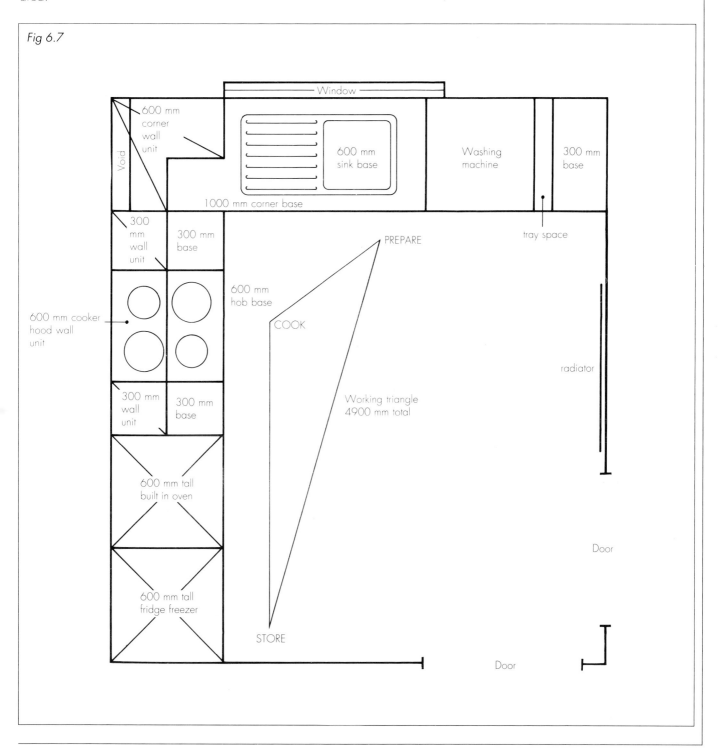

Fig 6.8 G-shaped kitchen (page 62)

Fig 6.9 'Island' kitchen (page 65-6)

Fig 6.8

Fig 6.9

The 'U-shaped' layout is a continuation of the L-shaped layout and is either used in bigger kitchens or in average sized kitchens where more than normal storage space is required. Again, the traffic flow will not interrupt proceedings in the kitchen.

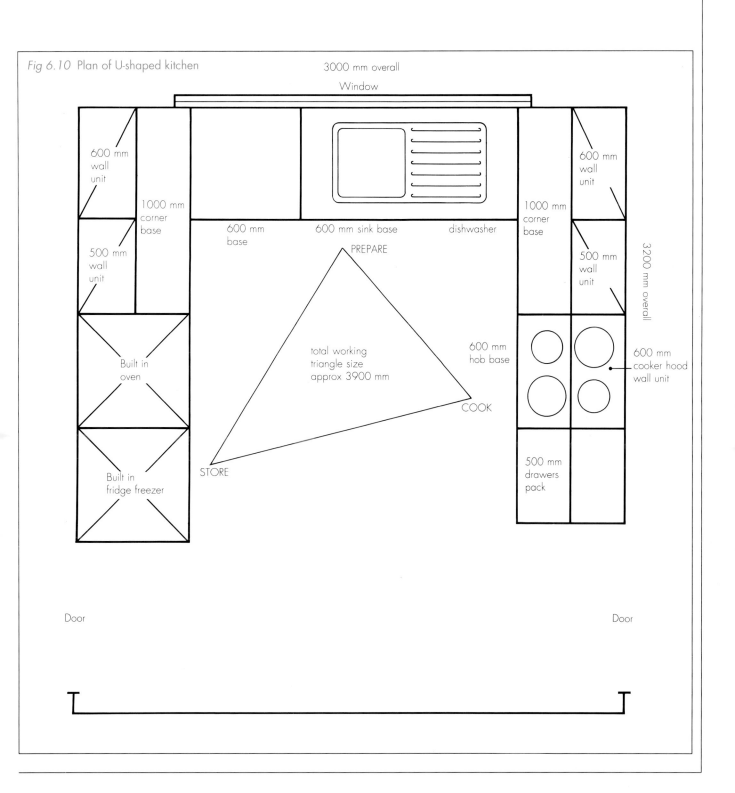

Fig 6.10 Plan of U-shaped kitchen

Again, the traffic flow will not interrupt proceedings in the kitchen. With very large kitchens the U-shaped layout can, however, necessitate unnecessary walking about to prepare food.

Therefore in bigger than average modern kitchens, the 'G-shaped' layout, which is an extension of the U-shape, is commonly used to eliminate the problem.

Here a projecting peninsular area can be used as a serving area and/or a breakfast bar or fixed dining area. This layout provides extra storage space and work surface area and completely encloses the working area, eliminating through traffic completely. In a very large kitchen the peninsular units can create a division to turn the room into a kitchen/diner.

Peninsulars in the kitchen/diner may also make use of display wall units as well as base units. These wall units can be supported on frames resting on the worktop, and this is an attractive feature when glass display wall units are used.

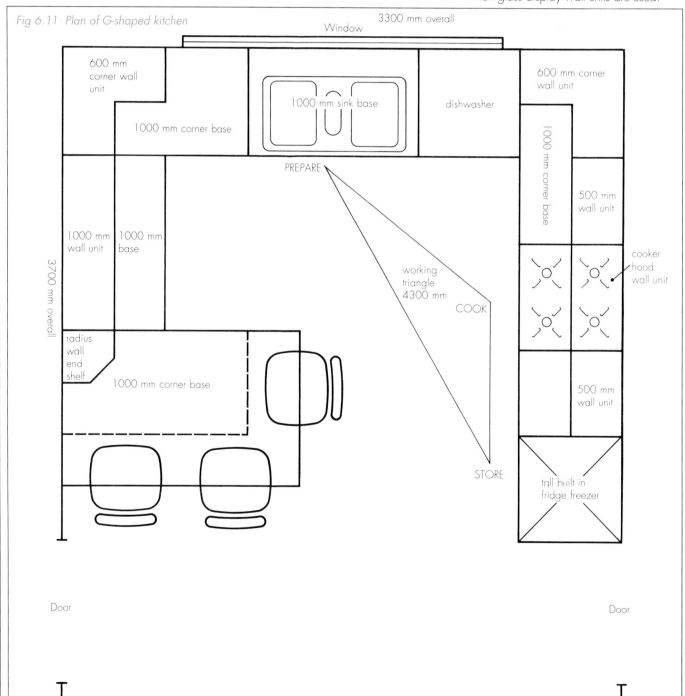

Fig 6.11 Plan of G-shaped kitchen

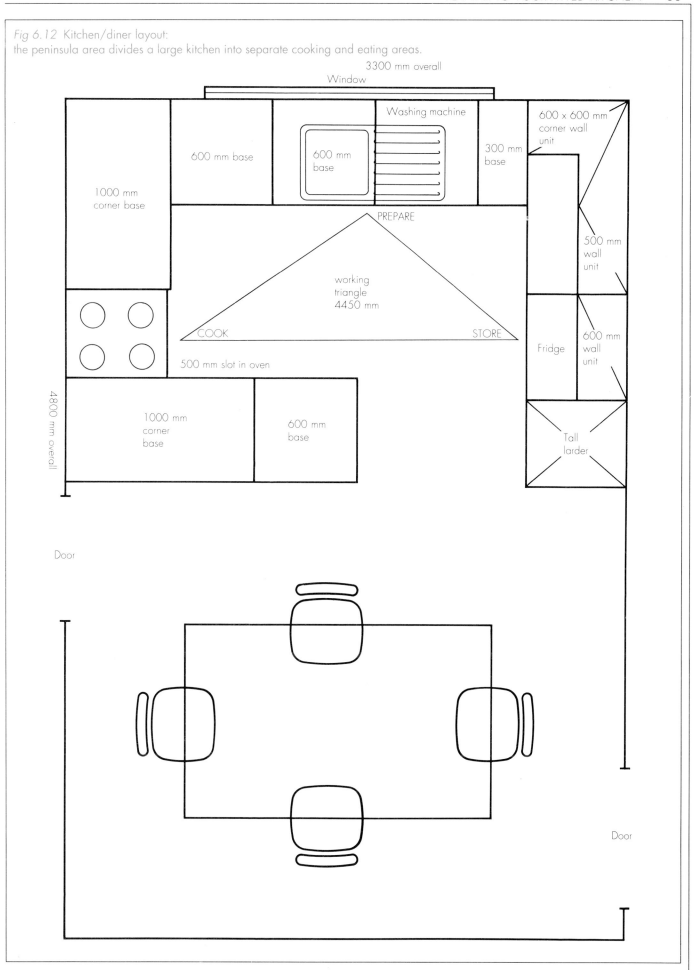

Fig 6.12 Kitchen/diner layout:
the peninsula area divides a large kitchen into separate cooking and eating areas.

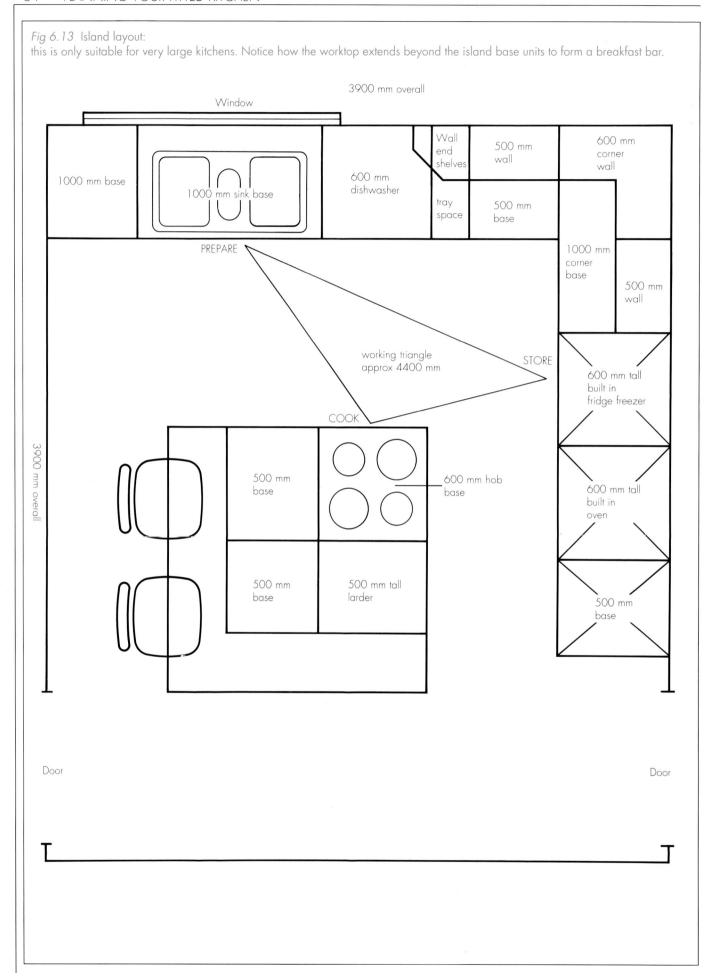

Fig 6.13 Island layout:
this is only suitable for very large kitchens. Notice how the worktop extends beyond the island base units to form a breakfast bar.

Finally we can consider in very large kitchens, the island layout where either an L- or U-shaped kitchen has an island of units in the centre. It is possible to incorporate the hob, or oven, or even the sink into the island of units and even combine these with a central island breakfast bar, if space allows.

One advantage of the island layout, with the hob set into the island units, is that a feature can be made of the extractor, by having a large purpose-built feature canopy suspended over the island, as described on page 25.

The logical work sequence

To achieve a well planned kitchen, it is wise to remember always that kitchens are for working in and should be planned to be efficient, safe and easy to use. The general public have now become more exacting in their demands when buying a fitted kitchen, and new ideas have added to the sophistication of the modern kitchen; but certain basic considerations still apply. When determining these basic considerations I am going to presume that the average kitchen is used mainly for the preparation of food, and the cleaning of equipment following that preparation. I will also presume that laundry is generally undertaken in the British kitchen (not many of us in the United Kingdom are lucky enough to have separate laundry facilities: continentals often site the washing machine in the bathroom, however). You may have particular requirements with regard to other activities taking place in the kitchen - there is the amateur wine-maker, to quote just one instance - so it is up to you to make the necessary adaptations.

In 1961 the Government published a report called Homes for Today and Tomorrow, which is usually referred to as the Parker-Morris Report. Since then, the Department of the Environment has published a guide to kitchen design and the British Standards Institute published BS3705 and BS6212 Part One, in the seventies and early eighties. These various reports have led to the theory of the 'working triangle', which I will endeavour to explain here.

Theoretically, the sequence of work in a kitchen is best illustrated as a straight line.

In the main, however, few kitchens allow siting of facilities in one straight line. In every kitchen there will be siting of the three major facilities:
a) Storage, e.g. larder and/or fridge,freezer
b) Preparation, e.g. sink and adjacent working surface
c) Cooking, e.g. oven,hob

If you look back at the previous pages, you will see that each type of kitchen layout illustration has a triangle in it. This is the work triangle, and represents the path you will take from the storage area, to the preparation area, then to the cooking area, and back to the storage area again. This work triangle should not be interrupted by doors - and the total distance of sides should be no longer than 6.6 metres and not shorter than 3.6 metres. If the sides are longer than 6.6 metres there will be lots of unnecessary walking about in the kitchen, and if this is done whilst in the process of carrying hot food, it may even be dangerous. If the sides are smaller than 3.6 metres the kitchen is cramped and will be difficult to work

in. Although I recommend you mentally absorb these recommendations, don't get too bogged down at the planning stage by trying to implement a perfect working triangle. The work triangle is something that you use to analyse the efficiency of the kitchen once it has been planned, whilst bearing in mind the siting of the three main areas of a) storage, b) preparation and c) cooking.

Now let us consider these three areas separately and in further depth. Once the general rules become clear to you, if you approach the planning of the kitchen with these rules in mind, the resulting plan will automatically include an efficient working triangle.

A   600   fridge under

B   600   sink base

C   600   autowasher

D   600   under oven & hob

E   300   base

F   600   base

G   600   cooker hob unit

H   600   wall unit

I   600   cooker hood unit

J   300   watt unit

Notice that thus the kitchen is planned so that the working sequence is from left to right in a straight line.

Food is stored in fridge and in unit above and prepared on the worktop over the fridge and in the adjacent sink bowl. Any mixing required can be done on the draining board or in the small space between the draining board and the adjacent hob.

We then move to the cooking area and finally we have a small amount of room on the right of the hob to serve

Thus the working triangle is in a straight line.

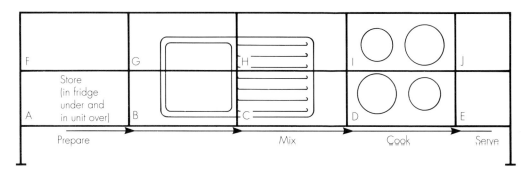

Patio door   Door

Storage area

Modern properties don't usually include a walk-in larder. Nowadays units and a fridge-freezer act as general food storage space. Upright fridge-freezers are more common than chest freezers, and if you do have a chest freezer or are considering one, remember that they are bulky and will occupy valuable floor space, and that when the lid is lifted it will foul any wall units placed above it. Consider siting a chest freezer in a garage or shed, under the stairs, or in any other convenient space, if you really need one. We have already looked, in the chapter about appliances, at the various types of fridges and freezers available to you. Remember too that tall units should be positioned on the end of a run of units so as not to interrupt the work surface. If you have a larger kitchen you can consider incorporating a built-under separate fridge and freezer and thus utilize working surface on top of them .

Tall larders are also best incorporated at the end of the run, and preferably next to the tall fridge-freezer if you have one. If space does not allow the use of a larder, the wall and base units will very adequately store foodstuffs instead.

Preparation area

This area consists of the sink and its adjacent working surfaces, which will be used to prepare food. The siting of this area is particularly important because most of the time spent in the kitchen is either spent preparing or washing up, which is of course done at the sink. Cast your eye back to the chapter on sinktops to confirm which type of sink will best suit your purposes and then consider where best to site it. This area will be the largest of the three main areas and should normally be positioned in front of the window to allow for good natural light plus a pleasant view whilst at work.

Dishwashers and washing machines should be situated next to the sink, where they can easily be plumbed in, and the sink itself should ideally be positioned away from a corner to allow the user to stand directly in front of it and even allow two people to work at the sink together, for example one washing and one drying.

In *Guidelines to Kitchen Planning* published by The Electricity Council in 1983, it is suggested that the preparation area consists of a sinkbowl with 500 mm of working space on either side (which may be incorporated into the draining board).

A good solution for the average householder would be to incorporate an inset sink and position the draining area over the washing machine or dishwasher, whilst trying to retain as much work surface on either side of the sinktop as possible.

I prefer to prepare food in a corner, because this allows me greater span of worksurface in one standing position: don't discount the use of a corner area with open worksurface as a preparation area, provided it is reasonably near the sink.

Cooking area

Always leave worksurface of at least 300 mm on either side of the hob. Obviously it is very inconvenient to have a hob up against a wall on the end of the run because handles of pots will be difficult to get at, and removal of pots and pans gets tricky if there is not adequate space on either side. Remember that a separate oven can be sited in a less busy area of the kitchen, since one does not stand at an oven as one does at a hob. Here again, as with the storage area, position tall units with built-in ovens at the end of a run.

Try to position the hob where a cooker hood may be installed above, and never site wall units directly over a hob. Cooker hoods should be at least 900 mm above a gas hob and at least 600 mm above an electric hob.

Site the hob or oven clear of doors which may cause draughts, swing open against the cook, or create traffic problems for the cook.

Last but not least, never locate an electric hob directly next to a sink or any water supply.

Obviously, not all kitchens conform to standard shapes and sizes; particularly, for instance, in properties where extensions have been added, or in old renovated or converted properties.

Conclusion

The previous layout descriptions and recommendations will arm you with enough information to stimulate your thought processes so that the actual drawing up of the kitchen plan doesn't become a tiresome process of trial and error. Correct thinking at this stage will also ensure that the final layout and the finished kitchen are as satisfactory as possible. If you sit down with pencil and paper without first considering the facts and consequent possibilities, then you will undoubtedly tire of drawing and redrawing plans that won't work. Do try, therefore, to absorb as much information as possible before you actually get down to the nitty-gritty of drawing up a plan.

Kitchen-planning is, as you will discover, merely an exacting game of logic. You are given four walls of pre-determined size, a set of rules which are no more than common sense, and a list of items which have to be set in the space between the four walls. There is always the best possible solution, and it is up to you to find it.

Stage 1: measuring walls and making an outline sketch plan

To help you measure and plan effectively you will need the following items: a 3- or 5-metre-long metric steel tape; a block of graph paper; a soft rubber; a pocket calculator and a propelling pencil with a 0.5 size lead, or a well sharpened ordinary pencil. You will, of course, need your scale rule, which you will find makes the planning process much easier.

All kitchen planners nowadays work to a scale of 1:20. In the good old days they tended to work 1:25 but nowadays 1:20 is universal, and all the plans in this book are presented in the same scale.

The first step is to make an accurate floor plan of your kitchen. This is where your tape measure comes in, and although a 3-metre tape is adequate a 5-metre tape is preferable, because so many kitchen walls are over 3 metres long; you don't want to be left in mid-air having run out of tape measure whilst you are measuring. If you are not yet conversant with metric measurements because you never learnt them in school, make sure that your measure has feet and inches on one side and is metric on the other.

This is a safeguard, because it is at the measuring stage that it is extremely important to be accurate; and it is at this stage that the professional kitchen planner 'mentally' checks off each wall as he measures it. That is, he will measure a length of wall and before drawing it to scale he will confirm in his own mind that the measurement he has taken is about right.

The majority of us will neither be so conversant with metric measurements nor be so adept at visualising length; therefore - particularly if you are more familiar with imperial measurements - measure each wall in imperial, mentally consider if the length sounds about right, and then take the measurement from the tape in millimetres.

Start in one corner and measure systematically all round the room until you are back to where you started. After you have taken each measurement, record it on the graph paper, using your scale rule.

Measure at a comfortable height with arms slightly raised, and when you are back to where you began in the corner you will soon see if you have made an error or if the walls are out of true, that is, not square, because your lines won't meet up. Remember to include windows and doors as you go, and mark them.

Next jot down where the gas outlet is, the cooker point is, and where the drainage for the sink is and mark them clearly on the outline. Also note any other obstacles such as gas meters, hot and cold water pipes, soil pipes and so on.

Now take a reading of the ceiling height and the window sill height and jot them down on your paper by the side of the plan.

Finally repeat the whole process of measuring once more to ascertain that your measurements are indeed accurate.

If there are any discrepancies between your two sets and they are only very minor, say 25 mm or so, then use the smallest measurement; because this will probably only mean that the walls are slightly unsquare, and this can usually be taken care of at the fitting stage.

Once you are convinced that you have your outline down correctly, you can move onto stage two.

The following pages show a typical kitchen plan building up by the same stages that you need to go through when planning your kitchen. The plans culminate in a finished kitchen exactly like the one in the photograph on page 93.

When planning your kitchen, use the scale rule supplied with this book and work on 1:20 graph paper. A sheet of this scale graph paper appears on page 96.

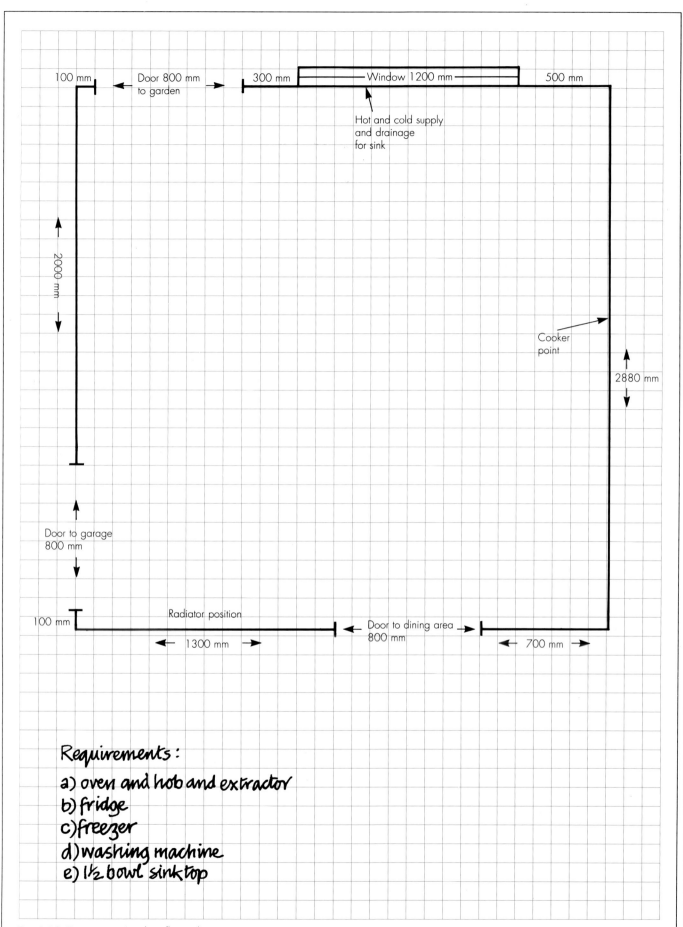

100 mm

Door 800 mm to garden

300 mm

Window 1200 mm

500 mm

Hot and cold supply and drainage for sink

2000 mm

Cooker point

2880 mm

Door to garage 800 mm

100 mm

Radiator position

Door to dining area 800 mm

1300 mm

700 mm

Requirements:

a) oven and hob and extractor
b) fridge
c) freezer
d) washing machine
e) 1½ bowl sink top

Fig 6.12 Drawing an outline floor plan.

Stage 2: checking appliance measurements and all relevant heights

On the same sheet of paper, make a list by the side of the outline of all the large appliances that will be going into your finished kitchen, and note their dimensions.

Now you must ascertain that appliances you have chosen will be suitable in terms of size. Check, if they are sited under a worktop, that they will indeed fit under. Usually these will be fridges, freezers, washing machines and dishwashers. Nowadays most appliances will fit snugly under the worktop, but there is always the old fridge that you want to hang on to for the time being which won't fit, so be careful. Pay particular attention to the widths of the appliances and jot these down. Next check that your units will not be positioned above the height of your windowsill. Check also that built-in appliances will be suitable for the apertures of the housings you wish to purchase, in height, width and depth. Here it would be a good idea to refer back to the chapter on appliances (pages 18-28). Finally, check the overall height of the units and ascertain that they will indeed be lower that ceiling height at all points. You may have to take account of stair wells or old beams, for example.

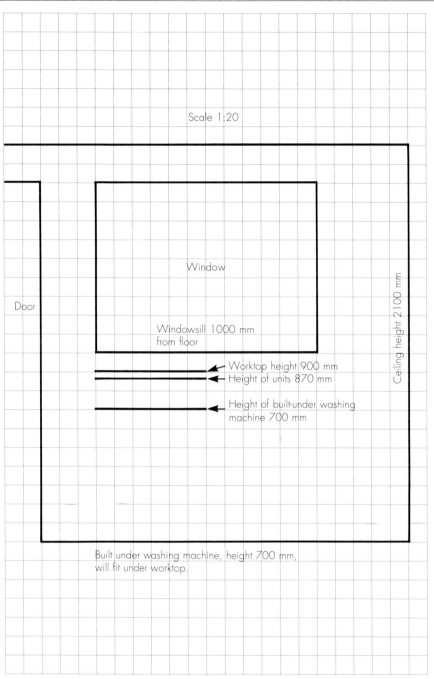

Fig 6.13 Calculating relevant heights.

Having done all this and recorded carefully and accurately all the relevant information, you are ready to begin drawing.

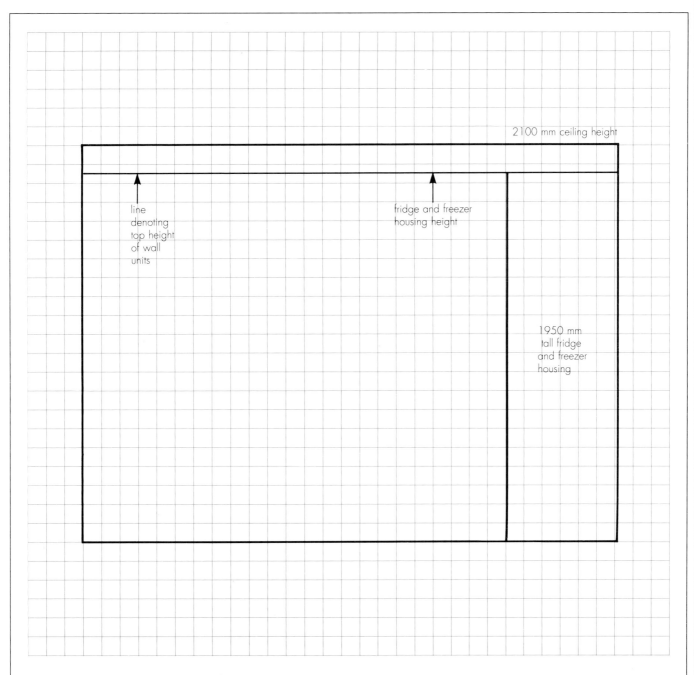

2100 mm ceiling height

line
denoting
top height
of wall
units

fridge and freezer
housing height

1950 mm
tall fridge
and freezer
housing

Fig 6.14 Positioning tall units and appliances

The best solution in this kitchen is a tall
built-in fridge and freezer stacked one
upon the other, to use less valuable floor
space than built-under units.

Since tall units always look best on the
end of a run we will position the fridge
and freezer as shown

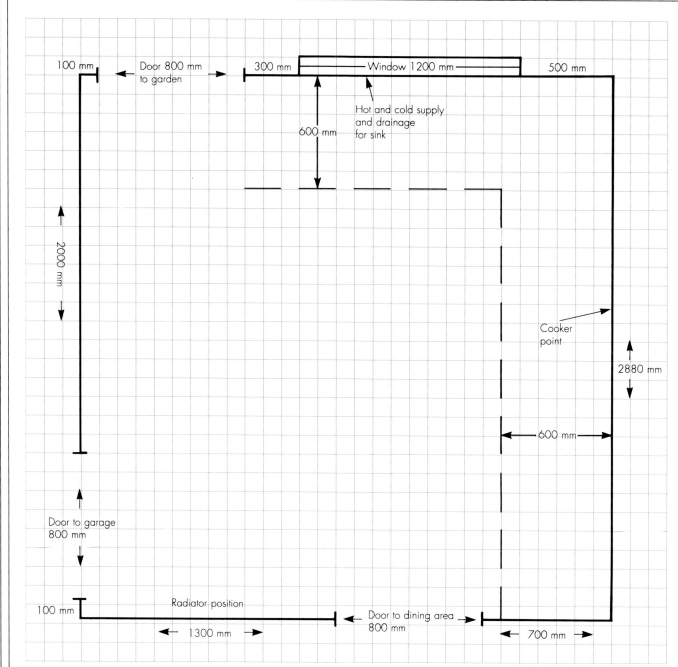

100 mm

Door 800 mm
to garden

300 mm

Window 1200 mm

500 mm

Hot and cold supply
and drainage
for sink

600 mm

2000 mm

Cooker
point

2880 mm

600 mm

Door to garage
800 mm

100 mm

Radiator position

Door to dining area
800 mm

1300 mm

700 mm

Fig 6.15 Putting in a working outline.

Stage 3: plotting the positions of units and appliances

Take your outline plan and draw a line 600 mm away from the wall, with the help of your scale rule, along each wall that you want to fill with units and appliances. This will give you an outline in which you can work.

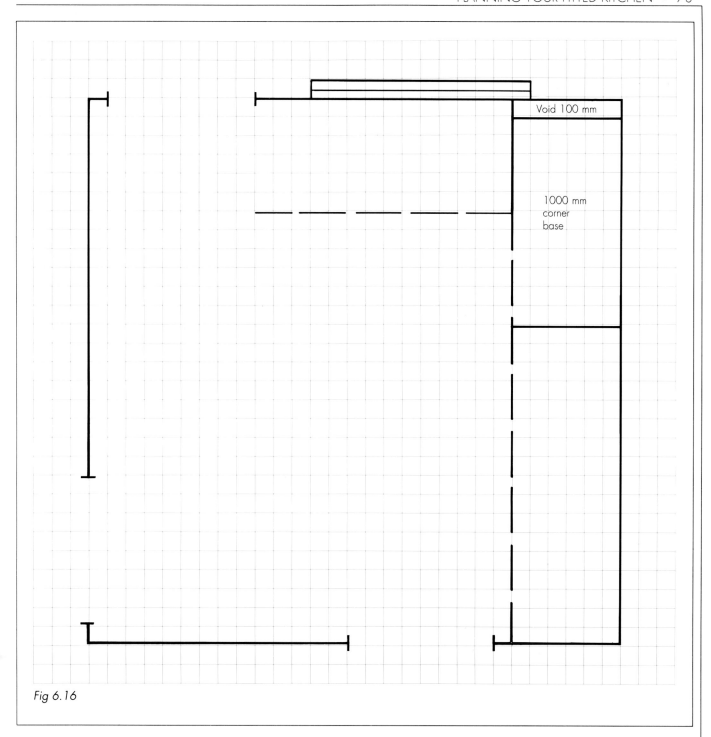

Fig 6.16

Next, having decided the most likely spot to put your oven, hob and sink, with reference to drainage and cooker supplies, begin in a corner by fitting in your corner base unit. Do make sure that you allow 1100 mm for your corner base, because even though the unit itself is only 1000 mm wide, it does in reality need 1100 mm of space, otherwise the door allowing access to the corner unit won't open. This is the first and most likely oversight on the part of novice kitchen planners.

Fig 6.11 The corner base is *not* positioned on the window wall, to leave space for sink and washing machine on that wall.

Void 100 mm

1000 mm corner base

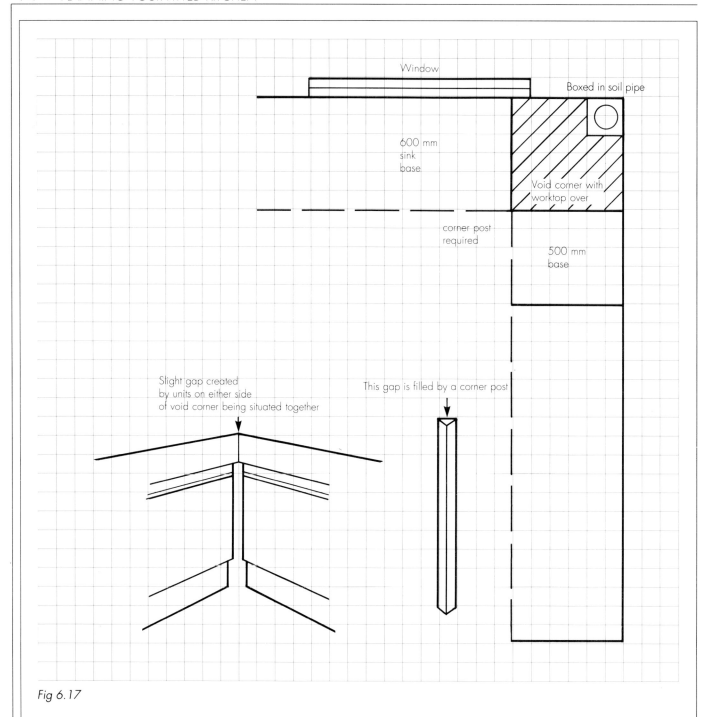

Window

Boxed in soil pipe

600 mm
sink
base

Void corner with
worktop over

corner post
required

500 mm
base

Slight gap created
by units on either side
of void corner being situated together

This gap is filled by a corner post

Fig 6.17

In cramped kitchens where a corner base will not easily fit it is possible to 'void off' a corner completely. This is useful where you have a soil pipe or other obstacle in the corner. If you do use a void corner then remember that you will need a 'corner post' - a tiny strip of wood-or melamine-faced chipboard, usually triangular in section - to fill the small gap that will remain between the two adjacent units.

Fig 6.17 If there had been a soil pipe in the corner we would have planned a void corner.

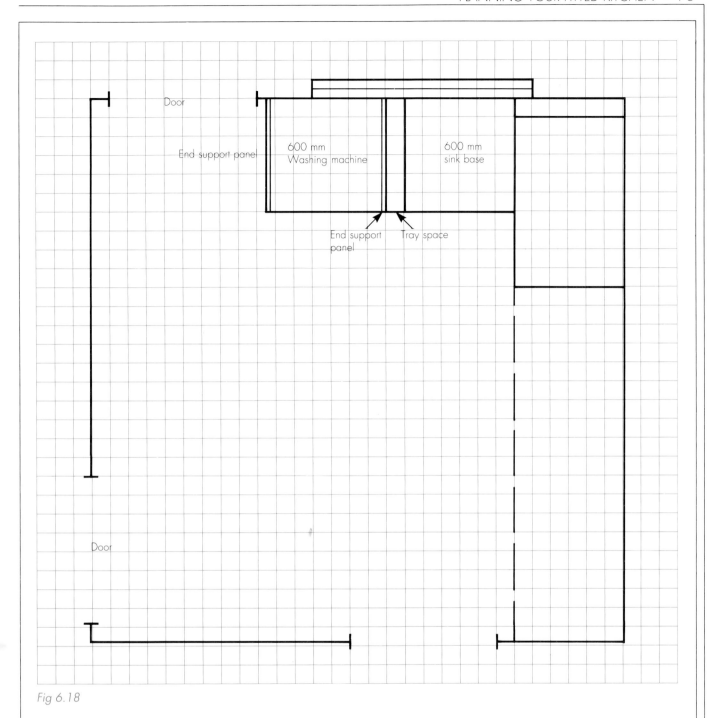

Door

End support panel

600 mm
Washing machine

600 mm
sink base

End support
panel

Tray space

Door

Fig 6.18

Because your sinktop position will be dictated by the position of your drainage in most instances, the next step is to move away from the corner and move towards the sinktop area. Remember to allow space as near the sinktop as possible for your washing machine or dishwasher, and remember to plot in unit widths as you are working to allow space for units to be included in between.

A sinkbase is a base unit 500 mm, 600 mm or 1000 mm wide. The size of unit which you use will be dictated by the type and size of the sinktop you wish to incorporate and the space allowed in the kitchen.

Fig 6.18 The sink and washing machine could be interchangeable, but this arrangement allows the sink to be centrally under the window.
Bringing the washing machine out to the end of the run has left about 120 mm of space into which we can incorporate a tray space. This gives tea towel storage usefully near the sink.

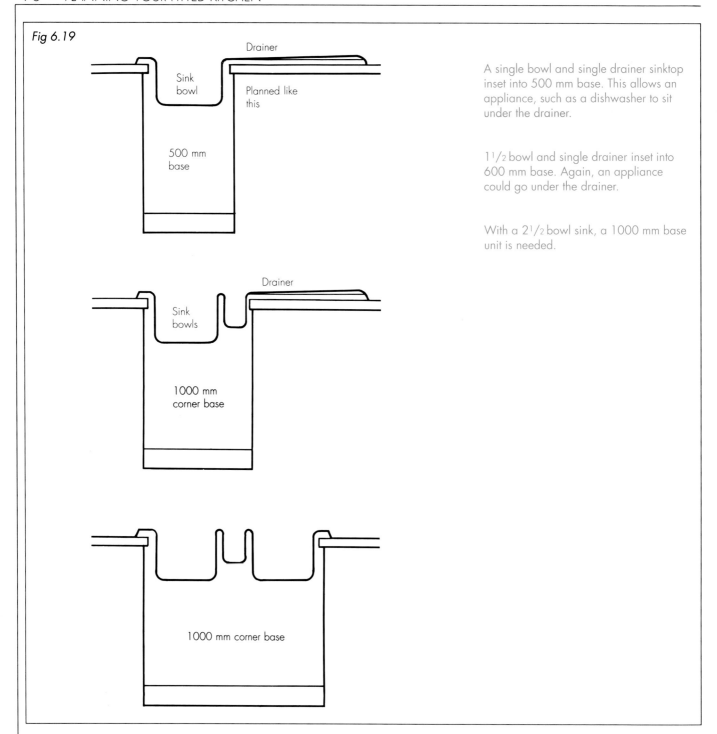

Fig 6.19

A single bowl and single drainer sinktop inset into 500 mm base. This allows an appliance, such as a dishwasher to sit under the drainer.

1 1/2 bowl and single drainer inset into 600 mm base. Again, an appliance could go under the drainer.

With a 2 1/2 bowl sink, a 1000 mm base unit is needed.

It is at this point that the alternative sinktop configurations which you have borne in mind since reading the section on sinktops will be whittled down to your final choice, by virtue of the fact that one will fit best in the space you now have.

Do check the manufacturer's dimensions again to ensure that your sinktop will indeed sit happily in a given base unit. You may have to come to terms with the fact that, much as you like a particular double-bowl sink, space will only allow you a single bowl. Remember too that right-handed people will work happily at a right-hand draining board and that left-hand drainers are for left-handed people; or to be planned only when there is no alternative space-wise.

Don't try to be too exact about situating wastes to connect to drainage. In fact, as long as you are to within a maximum of 2300 mm (which is a long way) away from drainage, then it is possible for the plumbing to cope with the rest. Just plan the sink as near to drainage as you can and you won't go far wrong.

Now that you have the sinktop and washing machine taken care of you can proceed to site the oven and the hob. Plot in the oven and hob in exactly the same way that you plotted the position of your sinktop, this time with reference to existing electric cooker or gas supplies. Remember that it is perfectly possible to re-site gas and electric cooker supplies if necessary; whereas re-siting drainage facilities is marginally more difficult and therefore more expensive.

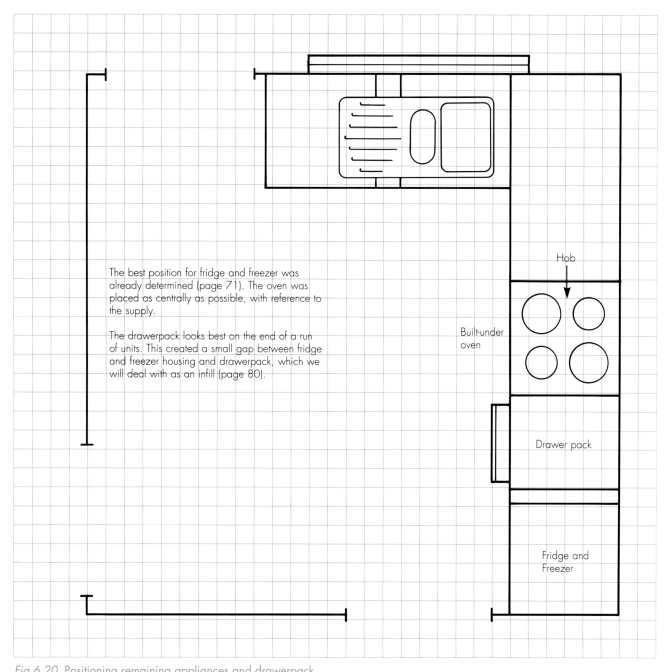

The best position for fridge and freezer was already determined (page 71). The oven was placed as centrally as possible, with reference to the supply.

The drawerpack looks best on the end of a run of units. This created a small gap between fridge and freezer housing and drawerpack, which we will deal with as an infill (page 80).

Hob

Built-under oven

Drawer pack

Fridge and Freezer

Fig 6.20 Positioning remaining appliances and drawerpack

You may have chosen a slot-in oven, or a built-under oven and hob and this will make planning at this stage a little easier, since you will be dealing with one positioning. If, however, you are incorporating a larger built-in oven with a separate hob, then consider the siting of the oven first, because it is the oven that needs the cooker supply if electric; whereas the hob is a lesser creature. If both oven and hob are gas then you will need to consider that both will need a gas connection, and so on.

Now consider filling in the spaces and

siting other electrical equipment such as fridges and freezers.

Use your scale rule and your calculator to check the preferable combinations of sizes and the possible positioning of units to fill the remaining available space. You do not necessarily need to draw in positions, but just check off the many possibilities so as to help you finally draw the best conclusions.

If you are using a 'doorline' range of units then you must also consider the drawerpack. All kitchens need drawers!

The drawerpack always looks better on the end of a run and will usually be 500 mm wide. So now try to plot in the position of the drawerpack.

Now you will find things coming together nicely like a jigsaw puzzle suddenly tends to do. In fact, as you progress, the whole process becomes easier rather than more complicated, because you are resolving a number of problems one after the other and in the relevant order. This means that solutions begin to dictate themselves as you go.

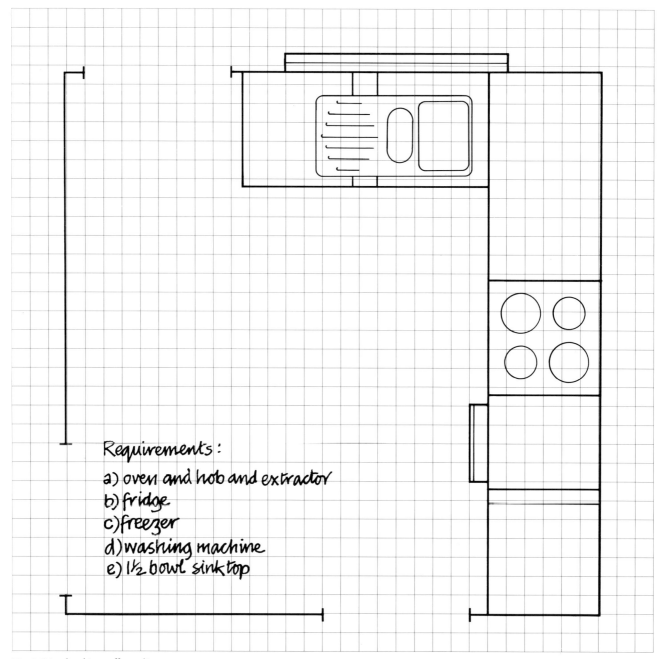

Fig 6.21 checking off appliances.

Requirements:
a) oven and hob and extractor
b) fridge
c) freezer
d) washing machine
e) 1½ bowl sink top

Do a quick check at this stage to make sure that you have taken account of all the various appliances which you have listed by checking them off on your list.

Now, with the aid of your calculator and scale rule, you are free to incorporate the base units which you would like or which you think you need, and which will fit best in the remaining spaces.

This is when you will get out your rubber and slightly reposition units and appliances accordingly. Bear in mind that the whole exercise is a type of learning process, in as much as you are at all times learning about the possibilities open to you in your kitchen. At this stage too, you may have a brainwave and the remaining spaces and sizes will suggest to you that you may incorporate something that hitherto you had not bothered to consider.

If, however, you have now got to the point where you have used an entire block of graph paper or worn out your rubber, go and have a cup of tea - you are taking things too seriously. But don't give up: you will find that after a while going about your daily business, solutions to some or all of the problems which you may have encountered will occur to you. If you have a really tricky kitchen problem that refuses to resolve itself after mature reflection, it may be worth calling in a professional.

Remember that all the work you have done will be far from wasted if you do this: you will still have far more understanding and control of the plan drawn up for you, and it might be a bit cheaper if you able to give the planner a clear and well-thought-out brief.

Finally, you will find that in nearly every kitchen you will have remaining - whatever you change and however much you replan - a minor gap of some description which will have to be filled. Here too there are basic principles involved. The first possible solution to try, in order to eliminate a nasty little gap, is to move everything toward one corner of the room so that gaps remain only on the end of a run of units.

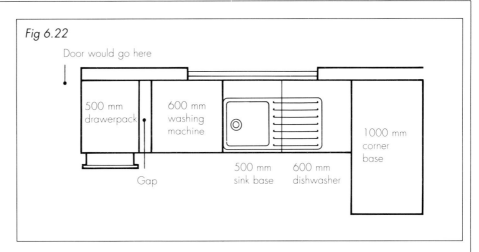

Fig 6.22

Door would go here

500 mm drawerpack

600 mm washing machine

1000 mm corner base

Gap

500 mm sink base

600 mm dishwasher

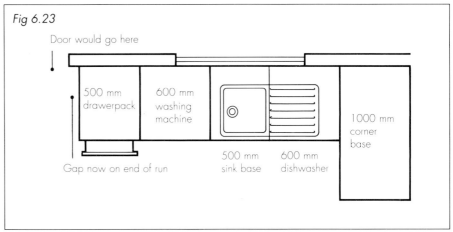

Fig 6.23

Door would go here

500 mm drawerpack

600 mm washing machine

1000 mm corner base

Gap now on end of run

500 mm sink base

600 mm dishwasher

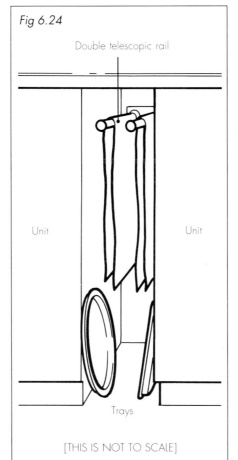

Fig 6.24

Double telescopic rail

Unit

Unit

Trays

[THIS IS NOT TO SCALE]

If this is not possible, in as much as it means leaving too large a gap on the end of a run of units, then you can cope in one of the following ways. Firstly you can use the gap for a tray space. A tray space is usually 300 mm wide when bought and is most often cut down in size by the kitchen fitter at the time of installation of the kitchen. In a well planned kitchen a tray space will be less than 200 mm wide when finished. A tray space becomes a useful item in your kitchen when juggled in near the sinktop and when combined with a pull out telescopic towel rail.

Fig 6.22 An unavoidable gap in a run of units.

Fig 6.23 Units moved up to eliminate gap.

Fig 6.24 A tray space

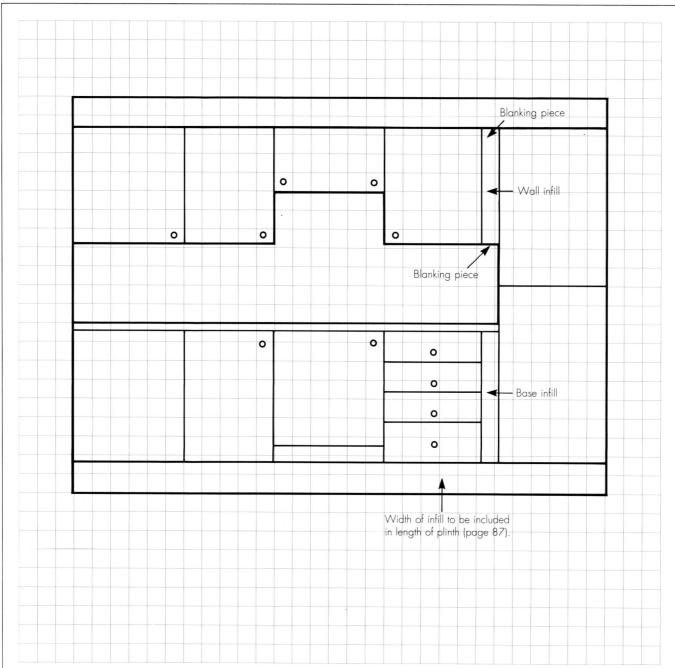

Fig 6.25 Planning in a base and wall infill.

Secondly, and particularly if you have more than one space in your run of base units, then do not be afraid to resort to the use of an 'infill'. Again, infills in a well planned kitchen will be under 200 mm wide.

Infills are constructed by either cutting down an extra matching door, or a sheet of veneer or laminate, and blanking off the given space with the cut down piece. Infills are best, if necessary, at the end of a run against a wall, but on odd occasions you will find that they do fall in the middle of a run of units. Don't be disheartened by the incorporation of an infill. Nearly all fitted kitchens have them.

The same principles apply to wall infills as to base infills. When you do order an extra door or a décor panel of given material for an infill, remember that for a base infill you will need extra plinth underneath it, and that for a wall infill you will need an underside and an upperside blanking piece, so organise spare carcase materials or ask your carpenter to supply them.

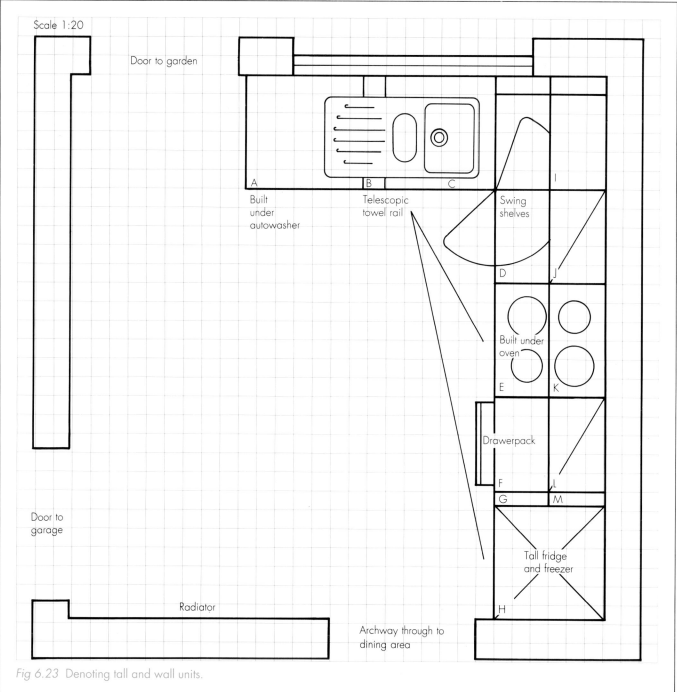

Scale 1:20

Door to garden

Built
under
autowasher

Telescopic
towel rail

Swing
shelves

Built under
oven

Drawerpack

Door to
garage

Radiator

Tall fridge
and freezer

Archway through to
dining area

Fig 6.23 Denoting tall and wall units.

You will have already plotted in your tall units with your base units. It is accepted practice to denote tall units on a scale plan with crossed diagonal lines. Do this next if you have tall units in your kitchen plan.

Now you can plot in the position of the wall units. This is easy as they merely slot into place directly above the base units and appliances that you have already planned, so that wall doors and base doors all line up nicely. Just as you began by drawing a line 600 mm away from your walls to plot in base units and appliances, now put in a line 300 mm away from your walls over your base units, to denote wall units.

As you denoted tall units with a crossed diagonal line, denote wall units with a single diagonal line.

Refer to the chapter on appliances, when you are plotting in your cooker hood; and turn back, too, to the section where the various heights of wall units are discussed, so that you remember how to plan tall units, standard wall units, tall wall units and cooker hood wall units in correctly. This is another place where novice kitchen planners almost invariably make a mistake. Too often a top box goes forgotten or a cooker hood wall unit is not the correct height.

Another very common first time and obvious error is the planning of wall units over windows, so when you come to a window, hold fire! A popular way of finishing off wall runs before a window is by including diagonal open wall shelving.

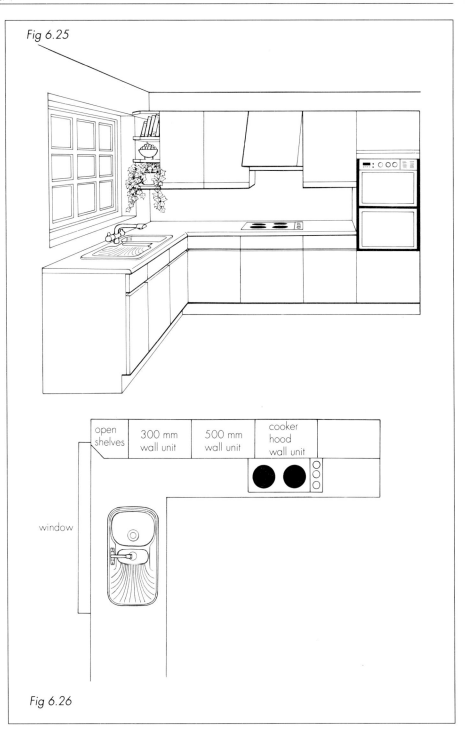

Fig 6.25 Diagonal wall shelving used to finish run of units before a window. In this case, a standard 300 mm wall unit would have over-hung the window in an unsightly manner. Open shelves overlapping a window are a more attractive solution.

Fig 6.26 Plan of above.

Now that your plan is complete, it's a good idea to check its feasibility with the help of children's chalk or masking tape. You can physically check over your proposals by chalking or taping measured lines in your kitchen.

Having ascertained that you are in business, so to speak, it now remains to obtain from your plan a list of materials that you will require.

You may feel at this stage that your plan is a bit rough, having been worked over considerably by now. A simple solution is to take some tracing paper and a fine-point felt tip and trace your plan out neatly.

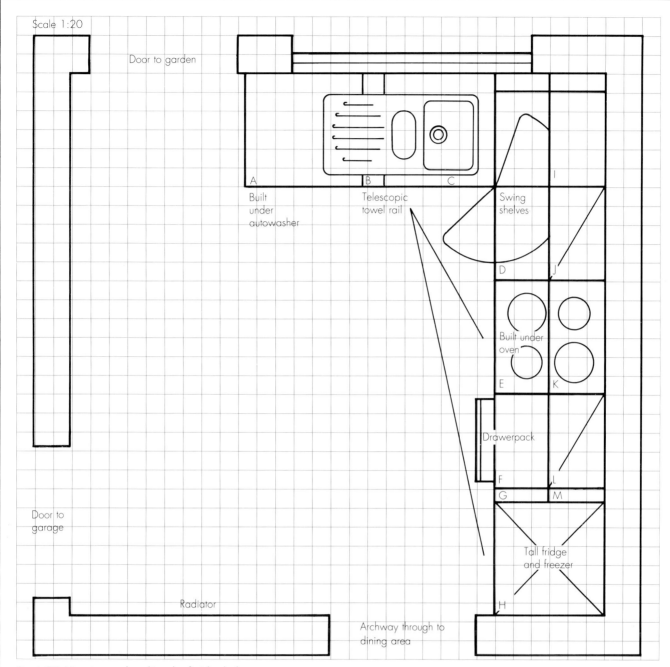

Scale 1:20

Door to garden

A Built under autowasher

B Telescopic towel rail

C

I Swing shelves

D

J

Built under oven

E

K

Drawerpack

F

L

G

M

Door to garage

Radiator

Archway through to dining area

Tall fridge and freezer

H

Fig 6.27 Naming and coding the finished plan

Now you can denote your hob and sink nicely using the conventional symbols as on your scale rule and also finish your plan nicely by denoting the thickness of your wall with an extra line 200 mm away from the outline

Show opening doors and the direction in which they will open; it's a good idea to mark them in their fully open position, to check that this won't cause any problems. Notice that windows are usually represented on a plan by a single line. Finally, to make the whole finished plan crystal clear, name and mark various items on it.

The next important step is to code each item on your plan alphabetically and in order. Start on the end of a run, work clockwise and code base runs first and wall runs in the second instance. Try to be extremely methodical because it is important at this stage not to miss an item out.

At the side of your completed plan, list the items one by one. This is important, not only to ensure that you will be purchasing everything you will need to complete your kitchen, but also because it will enable workmen to work easily from the plan.

Calculating quantities

With some of the items, for example, worktop and cornice, you will now need to calculate the quantities that you will require. It goes without saying that you will need to be reasonably precise in your calculations.

Worktops

The rule of thumb is to always oversize worktops. You can cut them down but you cannot very easily add to them. Remember above all that you will need worktops under your sink and hob if these are to be insets.

First of all you must plot in the position of your worktop joints. Worktop joints come in two varieties, 'in line' joints and 'corner' joints. An 'in line' joint is where a worktop, because of its length, has to be joined to another worktop on a straight run. The worktops are butted up together and either bolted and sealed or finished with a metal jointing strip.

A corner joint is where the worktops are cut and joined when they meet at a corner. Again you can have them cut, bolted and sealed (this is called a 'butt and scribe joint') or sealed with a special metal corner jointing strip.

It is fairly unusual to have an in line joint in your plan, but most kitchens will have corner joints. If you are sealing worktop joints with a corner jointing strip, don't forget to list the strips and make sure that they are the correct depth for the thickness of your worktops. If you are using 'butt and scribe' joints, then here again don't forget to list two bolts for every joint.

A common error in kitchen planning is to plan a hob or sink cut-out over or too near to a joint in a worktop. When you think about this it is totally impractical; firstly the strength of the worktop will be reduced, secondly the jointing strips are likely to become clogged with spillage from the hob or waste water from the sink, and thirdly the look of yourkitchen will be adversely affected - insets always look much better when surrounded by plenty of unbroken worktop. Plan worktop joints well away from cut-outs in worktops.

Now you must size your worktops. Take your scale rule and measure along each worktop run. Double-check this on your calculator by adding up the widths of all units and appliances over which the worktop runs.

I have already said that factory-cut worktops to particular sizes are difficult to cope with, since they must be exact to the millimetre. Therefore we will consider here only buying worktop blanks.

Obviously, there will always be some wastage when cutting worktops. Remember that if you are including butt and scribe joints in corners then you should allow 40 mm extra worktop for them. Again the keynote is to oversize rather than undersize.

When you have calculated how many worktop blanks you require, include in your list worktop edging strip, for edging cut unfinished ends of worktops.

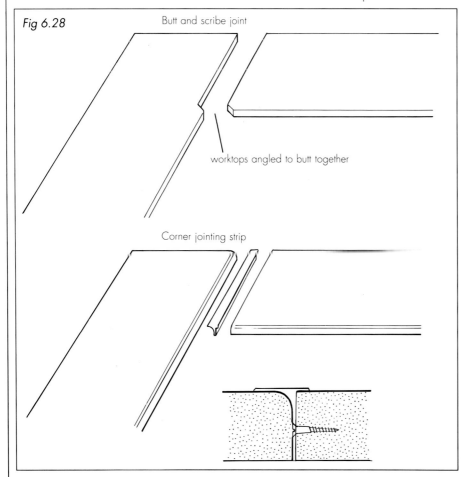

Fig 6.28

Butt and scribe joint

worktops angled to butt together

Corner jointing strip

Fig 6.28 Various worktop joints

Cornice

Cornice is the trim that runs along the tops of the wall and tall units to give the whole kitchen that 'finished' look. Cornice also tends to be supplied in 3-metre lengths. Use your calculator and scale rule just as you did when sizing worktops. The easiest way to calculate cornice is to add up the widths of the units along a run systematically allowing 10 mm for each mitre cut at joins, and 20 mm when two mitre cuts constitute a corner.

Take the total length required, including mitre cuts, and divide this by one length of cornice. This will give you the quantity of lengths of cornice that will be required. Again, always err on the generous side.

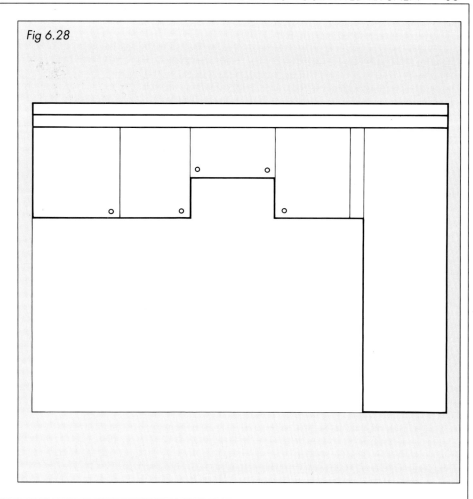

Fig 6.28

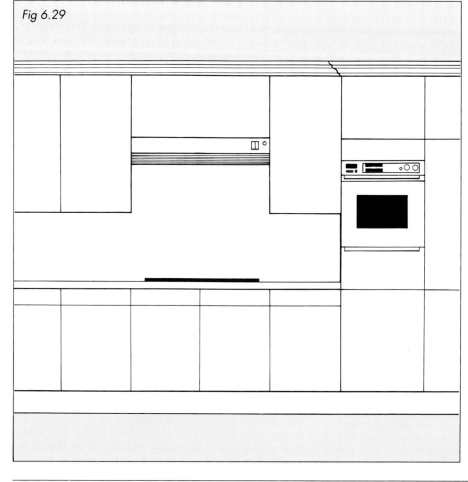

Fig 6.29

Remember to take cornice across the top of a cooker hood; if you are incorporating a feature canopy, however, then calculate the amount of cornice required to decorate the canopy.

Fig 6.28 Run cornice across a cooker hood wall unit as if it were a standard wall unit.

Fig 6.29 Cornice on a feature canopy

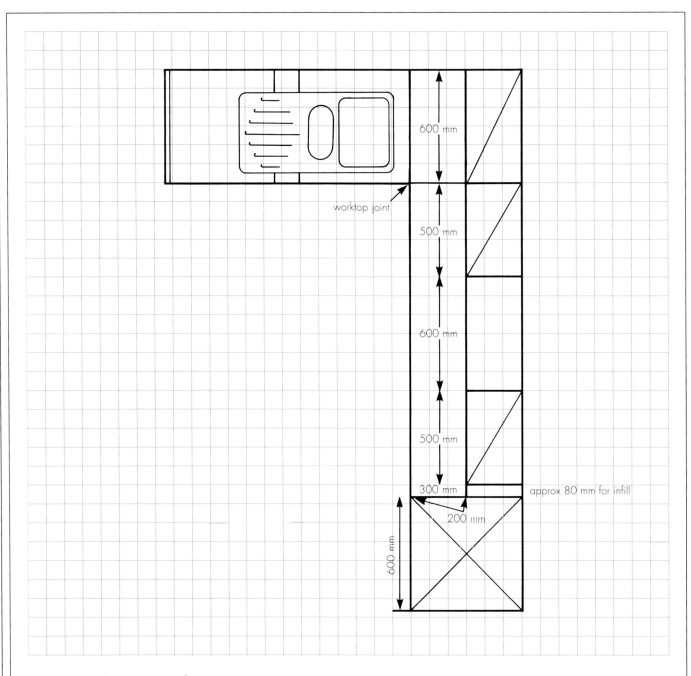

Fig 6.30 Calculating quantity of cornice.

Total cornice required 3580 mm. Thus we will require two lengths of cornice at 2500 mm per length. Notice that the worktop joint is set away from the sinktop rather than next to it, so the joint is stronger.

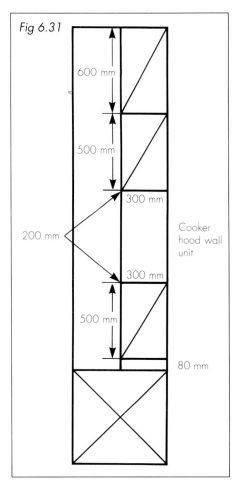

Fig 6.31

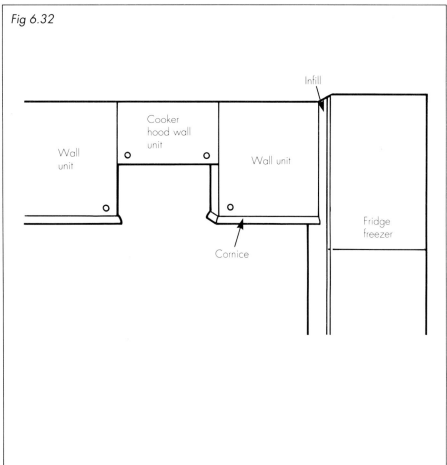

Fig 6.32

Lighting pelmet

Lighting pelmet, which runs across the bottom of your wall units and behind which your strip lighting for worktops can be concealed, is calculated in exactly the same way as cornice. Do remember that it runs back to the wall where you have a cooker hood, and finishes where the wall units meet tall units.

Continuous plinth

Some kitchen units will arrive with a plinth for each individual unit; some will arrive minus plinths and in this case continuous plinth is called for.

Continuous plinth finishes off your kitchen at the bottom just as cornice does at the top, so always opt for continuous plinth, if possible. Calculate lengths of plinth required in terms of runs of units. Plinth usually comes to you 2.5 metres or 3 metres long. Use your scale rule and your calculator and don't forget that you will require plinth across the bottoms of built-under and built-in ovens, dishwashers, washing machines, fridges and freezers.

Fig 6.31 Total lighting pelmet required: 2680 mm. This is just over 2500 mm so two lengths will be needed.

Fig 6.32 Lighting pelmet, unlike cornice, finishes where it meets tall units.

2 × end support panels
600 mm built under washing machine
1 integrated door or decor panel
    for washing machine
Tray space
600 mm base unit
Waste bin
1000 mm corner base unit
    (including corner post)
Swing shelves
600 mm built under single oven housing unit
Built under single electric oven
Electric hob
500 mm drawerpack
Cutlery insert
300 mm base door only
    (for use as base infill)
600 mm tall fridge and freezer housing
Built in larder fridge
Built in freezer
2 × integrated doors or decor panel
    for fridge + freezer
600 mm standard wall unit
2 × 500 mm standard wall unit
600 mm cooker hood wall unit
600 mm extractor
300 mm wall door only
    (for use as wall infill)
1½ bowl + drainer inset sinktop
Basket accessories and chopping board
    for sinktop
Wastes for sinktop
Monobloc sink mixer tap
2 × worktops 3000 long × 600 wide × 30 deep
1 × worktop corner jointing strip
2 × 2500 mm lengths of decorative cornice
2 × 2500 mm lengths of lighting pelmet
2 × 2500 mm lengths of continuous plinth

Corner ovens and breakfast bars

Having added to your list the quantities of the above items that you will require, you are now ready to obtain quotes, or indeed, place an order at the outlet of your choice. Before we move on to discussing placing orders and taking delivery of your kitchen, it may be pertinent to consider a few more complicated planning situations which are more tricky to cope with, for those of you who have sailed through the previous planning stages.

Corner ovens

This can be good way of making a feature in a large kitchen. The hob can be put over a built-under oven. If you are incorporating a tall built-in oven and hob then you can substitute a 600 mm base unit under the hob instead. Do not forget that you will need two corner fillets on either side of the base unit or oven housing and that the easiest way of coping with wall units and extractors is by subsequently planning in a canopy made to suit on site.

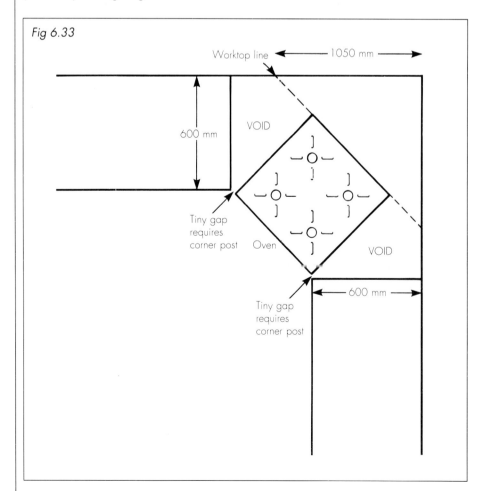

Fig 6.33

Fig 6.33 When planning in a corner oven and hob—or just a hob over a 600 mm base unit in a corner—remember that you need the corresponding amount of wall space free of windows to put a canopy extractor over the hob. Moreover, the canopy does need to have wall units on *both* sides of it to look balanced.

Fig 6.34 A breakfast bar can make use of many awkward spaces in small kitchens.

Fig 6.35 Here a niche in the wall is utilised, with worktop cut to size and the end cut diagonally to avoid a sharp corner. High-level stools store under it easily.

Fig 6.34

Breakfast bars

The ways of dealing with breakfast bars are practically limitless. I have included here a few simpler versions. One simple way of constructing a breakfast bar is by leaving a space between units and merely running the worktop across the space; you can store high level stools for use at the bar under the worktop.

Fig 6.35

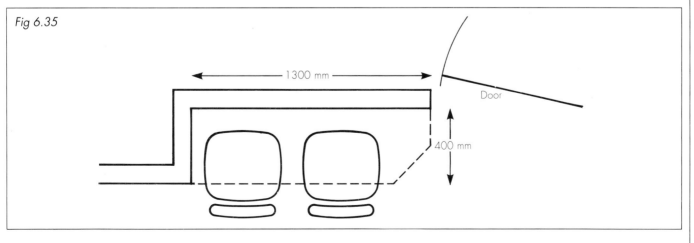

Fig 6.36 Worktops can be cut and bracketed to the back and side of a corner base unit to make a low-level breakfast bar to use with chairs.

Fig 6.37 Drawing of low-level breakfast bar.

Fig 6.38 A bar for use with high-level stools can be made with wide worktop on a corner base in a peninsula.

Fig 6.39 Drawing of high-level breakfast bar.

A simple peninsular breakfast bar can also incorporate high-level stools or use table-top-height additions of extra worktop for bench-style seating.

Notice from the diagrams that 300 mm depth of worktop space is the minimum required for happy eating. In terms of length 1300 mm of top will happily seat two or three people side by side.

Obviously the size of your breakfast bar, i.e. how many base units you employ in the design, will be dictated by the size and shape of your kitchen, and by how many people you wish to seat at once. The illustrated examples should fit into most average or above-average sized kitchens, and will seat four people at once at a pinch.

When calculating worktop for breakfast bars remember that both sides of the worktop, if in one piece, will need to have postformed edges. The same applies to simple peninsular units with worktop.

Most worktop manufacturers provide 3-metre or 3.5 metre-blanks in the following sizes, to provide for breakfast bars: 3000 x 600 mm worktop with a single postformed edge; 3000 x 640 mm worktop with double postformed edges; 3000 x 900 mm worktop with double postformed edges.

Fig 6.36

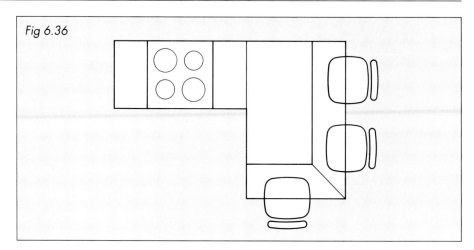

Fig 6.37

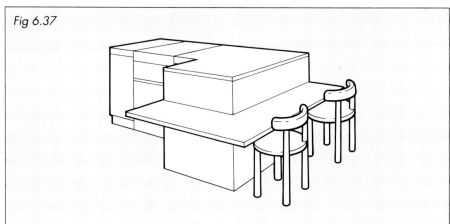

Fig 6.38

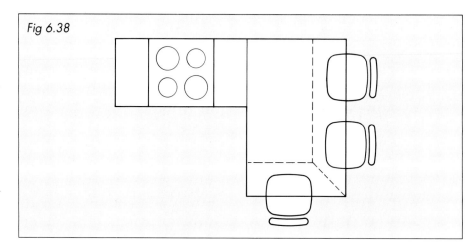

Fig 6.39

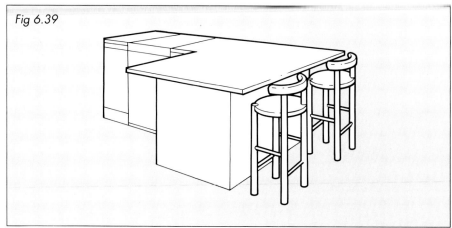

DELIVERY AND FITTING

By now you will be armed with a well thought out plan and an itemised list of requirements, but before you place any orders there are just a few more rules to be observed.

First of all always obtain a written, itemised quotation and check it off against your listings to ensure that nothing has been forgotten and that the individual prices are in all cases reasonable. When you are satisfied that all is well then enquire about methods of payment. Do you for instance need to put down a minimum deposit? When do you pay the balance and how? If again all is agreed and in order then you can steam ahead.

When your kitchen arrives, however, never take for granted that all is still well. Check and double-check that each individual item is present and correct and check receipts (which should also be itemised) in case a problem with an item does turn up at a later stage.

Fitting

Finally, just a quick word about kitchen fitting. If you are employing a kitchen fitter then try to do so on the basis of recommendation from someone you know. A pefectly well planned kitchen can be ruined by bad fitting, so try to get to see some of the fitter's previous work too. It is still a risk taking someone even on recommendation, unless you are sure of your informing source, and have seen some of their work for yourself.

If, on the other hand, you are an ardent do-it-yourselfer and want to fit the kitchen yourself, you will have the great advantage of being intimately aware of how the kitchen is designed so you will know exactly what fitting problems to cope with and at what stage in the proceedings (to say nothing of the self-satisfaction you can anticipate).

Fitting your kitchen yourself if far from impossible and I am assured by professional kitchen fitters that anyone with a modicum of common sense can cope, provided that they take the time to do it properly. It is important to approach kitchen fitting systematically, and the keynote of the exercise is 'upright and level'; you will need to make good use of a spirit level throughout.

Because walls and floors are never truly level and flat, but, on the other hand, units are constructed as if they were, a major part of the fitter's job is to compensate for irregularities by either 'packing' units up and out, or 'scribing' units (i.e., cutting them down), hence the spirit level. Whether packing or scribing, the aim is to arrive at a positioning of a unit that is level and vertical. With base units, there may be wedges for packing, and some units have adjustable feet: if they have neither you can use bits of quarterply formica or some other suitable material of a uniform thickness.

Obviously, before you begin to assemble and position any units at all, you must strip out your old kitchen. Here again work systematically and methodically. Do not just crowbar old units out, but undo the screws that are holding the old units together and to the wall. Strip everything out bar the sink.

Once you have stripped the kitchen, you can, using your spirit level and chalk, mark the positioning of the units, beginning with the base units. In extreme cases you may have to prepare the walls a little by sanding and chiselling to render them as flat as possible.

When installing units, always begin in a corner, and start with the base units. To assemble self-assembly units, refer to the manufacturer's assembly instructions. A typical set of instructions will take you through the following stages, but first use a check-list to ensure that all the relevant bits are indeed present and correct.

Fig 7.1 *Fig 7.1* Putting together a self-assembly wall unit

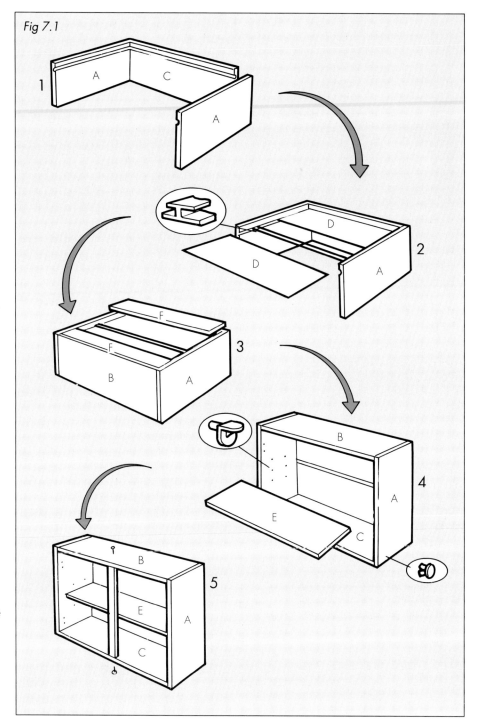

To assemble a self-assembly wall unit

1. Attach the two side panels to the bottom panel with the screws provided.

2. Slot the back panel into position between the side panels.

3. Attach the top panel.

4. Attach the back rails (through which you will screw the unit to the wall).

5. Insert the shelf.

6. Insert the centre post, if there is one. On larger wall units there may be one to keep the unit rigid.

7. Secure the unit to the wall through the back rails, with the screws that are normally provided, making sure it is level and in the correct position.

When you have secured one unit to the wall you may secure the next one and then secure each unit to its neighbour.

Incidentally, only when all the units are in position do you attempt to hang the doors. Putting on doors is the very last thing you will do.

Worktops should not present a great problem, provided you have the use of a jigsaw. They are secured to the base units from the underside using screws that are provided with the base units. Whilst fitting worktops, you may systematically plumb and position an inset sink. Again I am assured that plumbing a sink is a relatively straightforward operation; however, the consensus of opinion is that when it comes to gas and electricity it is time to call in the experts.

I have here merely furnished you with enough information to enable you to decide if you would like to attempt the fitting of the kitchen yourself. There are one or two books available which concentrate solely on the fitting of kitchens, if you feel you do want to have a bash yourself.

If you decide, on the other hand, that you would prefer to leave it to the experts, be wary of allowing the people who supplied the units to do the fitting as well, since this can be very expensive.

Whatever your active role has been in achieving your finished fitted kitchen, if you have followed the procedures set out in this book you should have been able to acquire a well-thought-out, well-planned kitchen that not only reflects your personal tastes, but also is an intelligent, good-value-for-money buy.

Fig 7.2 The finished kitchen – based on the plans on pages 69–83.

INDEX

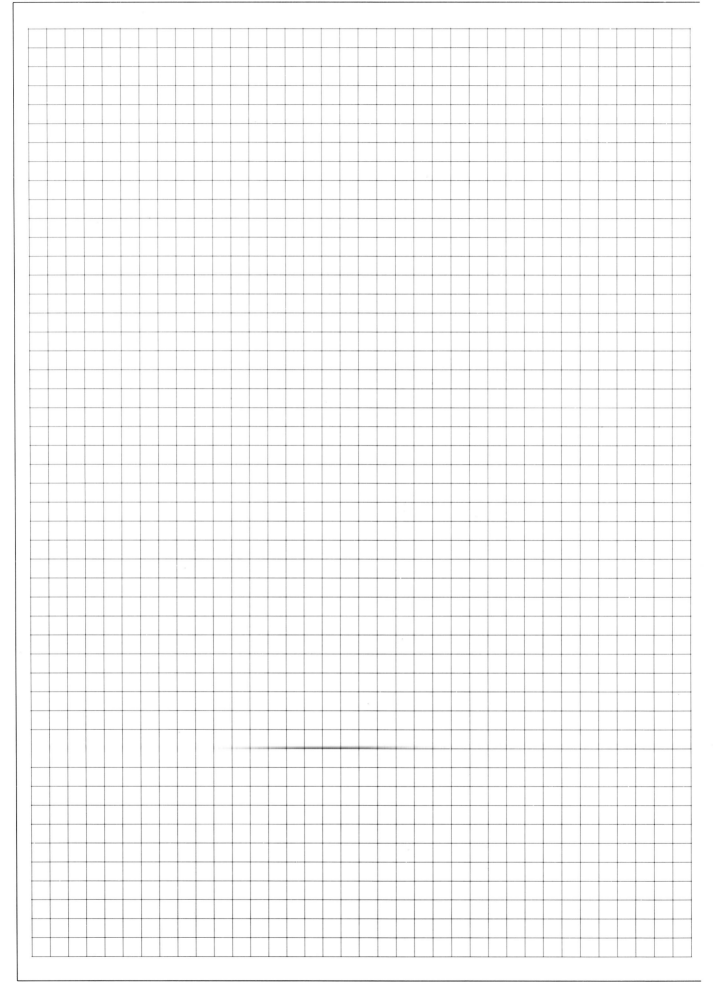